PSYCHOANALYSIS
OF THE SEXUAL FUNCTIONS
OF WOMEN

Helene Deutsch

PSYCHOANALYSIS
OF THE SEXUAL FUNCTIONS
OF WOMEN

Helene Deutsch

edited and with an introduction by

Paul Roazen

translated by

Eric Mosbacher

Karnac Books

London   1991   New York

To the Memory
of J. David Greenstone

First published in 1991 by
H. Karnac (Books) Ltd.
58 Gloucester Road
London SW7 4QY

Distributed in the United States of America by
Brunner/Mazel, Inc.
19 Union Square West
New York, NY 10003

British Library Cataloguing in Publication Data

Roazen, Paul
  Psychoanalysis of the sexual functions of women.
  1. Women. Sexuality
  I. Title
  306.7082

  ISBN 0–946439–95–8

Printed in Great Britain by BPCC Wheatons Ltd, Exeter

CONTENTS

PREFACE

Sigmund Freud believed that his psychology represented universal and revolutionary findings about human nature. As a practical matter he knew that the clinical origins of his theories could threaten the wider acceptance of their objective status; and he at times acknowledged that each era, as well as individual countries and social groups, could be expected to exhibit their own unique features. Yet as an issue of scientific principle the founder of psychoanalysis aimed to bypass the superficialities of so-called common sense. The older he became, and the broader his following grew, the more he believed that his hypotheses had been confirmed by qualified independent observers. From the outset Freud had sought to lay bare the basic self-deceptions that characteristically

I am immensely grateful for the help in reading this material offered by Dr Elaine Borins, Dr June Engel, Dr Carol Nadelson, Dr Malkah Notman, Dr Michael Rogin, and Dr Irvine Schiffer.

disguise the depths of the unconscious that unite all human beings.

By now Freud's immense stature in intellectual history is secure. At the same time, it is only too clear to us today that, born in 1856, he was inevitably working within the confines of his own culture. Consider a casual clinical aside from a 1909 essay: 'supposing . . . that a hysterical woman has a phantasy of seduction in which she is sitting reading in a park with her skirt slightly lifted so that her foot is visible . . .' (Freud, 1909a [1908], p. 231). Such a reminder of how differently women dress today points to the larger question of how different Freud's world was from our own. The civilization of old Vienna, one of the focal points in the spiritual history of the West, has disappeared long since.

Indeed, it would be mistaken to assume that old-world culture was in any way lacking in sophistication when it came to an appreciation of the full possible complexities of psychological conflicts. The ways in which people dress or talk in public are only bridges to an understanding of how they behave or feel. In fact, in contrast to some of our own conformist notions about establishing the differences between the sexes, the milieu of early psychoanalysis was far more enlightened than most other periods in history about the inevitability of human diversity (Roazen, 1989, pp. 43–48). One of the sources of Freud's own contempt for American life, for example, was its naive optimism about human improvement, as well as what he saw as a repressive and guilt-laden outlook on sexuality.

It is easy to be misled in such matters by outward appearances. Popular mythology would have it that late-Victorian society was marked by an arbitrary suppression of natural human impulses. Manuals about sexual performance are now abundantly available; accounts of private fantasies have been popularized; protest groups of homosexual 'deviants' are commonplace; and therapists (even surgeons) have tried to alleviate specific sexual dysfunctions or anomalies. Of course science has taught us a great deal about the biochemistry of sexuality since

Freud's time, and genuinely new psychotherapeutic approaches have been introduced. Still, it is highly questionable whether in the realm of such intimate subjects there has been anything approaching what might be called moral progress.

Much of what passes for enlightenment in our own day would by turn-of-the-century European standards have seemed vulgar, if not childish. Sex may be degraded as an athletic pursuit under various guises; the Kinsey statistics may have had a liberating effect, but they also reflect a depersonalized, mechanical outlook on sexual life (Trilling, 1957; Robinson, 1976). And the quest for public sexual identities and preferences can be looked upon as a new way of freezing human potential into a fresh set of stereotypes. Without thinking that sex must always be viewed in a sacred light, it is still possible so to divorce physical acts from emotional significance as to succeed in disguising or debasing sexuality under the banner of emancipation.

Freud was working in a context radically unlike our own; and to the degree that his world was different from ours, an examination of the implications of some psychoanalytic ideas can hope to offer an alternative to our contemporary standards. Although aspects of his system may sound puritanical, in reality Freud could sometimes be so flexible as to appear cynical: the problem with masturbating, he is reported to have once remarked, is that one has to know how to do it well (Hitschmann, 1954).

From today's perspective Freud as a man was far more open, and interesting, than many of his idolatrous followers have publicly wanted to represent him. Despite what some, including Pope Paul VI, may have thought, Freud was never a proponent of anything like free love. He accepted marriages of convenience, for example, and did not necessarily frown upon couples who did not have intercourse with one another. To him, companionship was something special in its own right. If Freud could go to what some might think unacceptable extremes, doubtless the divorce rate in North America would be less if people had lower expectations about married life, or tolerated more readily old-fashioned extra-marital arrangements.

Human diversity is a precious aspect of civilized life and ought not to be sacrificed on the altar of some transient definitions of normality (Roazen, 1989, pp. 319–327). Freud himself thought that however self-damaging neurosis might be, it was also a sign of superior human worth. The absence of suitable guilt feelings would indicate what he would regard as inner emptiness. For example, one of his married pupils, after the conclusion of treatment, was carrying on an affair away from home; when his wife visited town, this analyst suddenly found himself impotent with her. Freud, when consulted by the pupil distraught over the results of analytic therapy, took the occasion to congratulate his disciple on this sign of decency (Kardiner, 1977, p. 74). To Freud's way of thinking a gentleman's unconscious would, with a woman he had betrayed, interfere in such a way.

Freud's ideas, like those of other psychologists, were a reflection of his own autobiographical self-understanding; but his concepts were also designed to cope with the clinical phenomena as these presented themselves to him. Although his patients were generally not as disturbed as, for instance, the trans-sexuals who form the basis of some current gender identity theory (see for example, Stoller, 1974), the people who engaged in his form of treatment were suffering from complaints that were more severe than found in a comparable psychoanalytic population today. Whereas in the mid-1960s in a city like Boston, Massachusetts, the most common 'symptom' among those allowing themselves to become patients (at reduced fees) for analysts-in-training was an inability to complete a Ph.D. thesis, throughout the 1920s the most frequent diagnosis at the out-patient clinic of the Vienna Psychoanalytic Society was impotence (Hitschmann, 1932, p. 252).

Freud's earliest ideas were cast in the perspective of the male, because they were based on his self-analysis, and this remained largely true even though most of his early

cases were women. One of the less convincing aspects of
Freud's early thinking was his view of female development, which led to some of the earliest fundamental critiques of psychoanalysis (see, for example, Miller, 1973).
What may have looked like a devaluation of women was
matched by a tendency to idealization, and Freud dis-
played nineteenth-century gallantry towards them. Yet a
wide gulf separated his theories from his clinical practices.
It is too easy now to overlook how far ahead of himself
culturally Freud was in treating men and women as
equals. To one highly artistic male patient, Freud specifically linked creativity to femininity. 'You are so feminine
you cannot afford to let it out,' Freud told him, and Freud
intended this interpretation as a compliment.

The limitations of Freud's bias were undoubtedly
checked by the logic of his conviction that all people are
inevitably and innately bisexual. Since Freud was an eth-
ical thinker as well as a scientist, recent embryological
research on dimorphism (Sherfey, 1972, pp. 42–48) cannot
ultimately settle the matter, biologically, for or against his
approach. Moral concepts on behalf of androgyny are as
humanly relevant as any appeal to early 'nature.' A theory
of bisexuality encourages tolerance rather than cultural
preconceptions about maleness and femaleness.

In 1899 Freud wrote that he was accustoming himself 'to
the idea of regarding every sexual act as a process in which
four persons are involved' (Freud, 1954, p. 289). The notion
that two people in bed can really be looked upon, in terms
of the unconscious, as four should do something to dispel
the myth that Freud was more staid than we are today.
The existence of feminine components in men and a masculine side to women was, therefore, entailed in some of
Freud's most basic beliefs. In terms of the history of psychoanalytic theories, however, it was only in the 1920s
that the understanding of female psychology began to
match that of the male.

Helene Deutsch's *Psychoanalysis of the Sexual Functions
of Women,* which appeared from Freud's Vienna publishing

house in 1925, was the first book by a psychoanalyst on female psychology. Karen Horney reviewed it in a lengthy essay at the time (Horney, 1926), and the book is a classic text in the development of psychoanalytic thought about women. Although Freud, who rarely mentioned the writings of his pupils, explicitly cited this book on two prominent occasions, in 1925 and in 1931 (Freud, 1925j, p. 258; 1931b, p. 242), it has not until now been translated into English. The early professional literature could not fail regularly to refer to *Psychoanalysis of the Sexual Functions of Women* (see, for example, Bonaparte, 1935, p. 325; Brierley, 1932, p. 437; Fenichel, 1931, p. 166, 1933, p. 567, 1945, pp. 90, 173, 175, 411; Horney 1967, pp. 55, 148; Jones, 1961, pp. 441, 444; Klein, 1950, p. 208, 1960, pp. 271, 289, 306, 309; Lampl-de Groot, 1948, p. 181; Payne, 1935, p. 28; Rado, 1928, p. 315; Reich, 1975, p. 263; Searl, 1938, p. 52; for rare recent citations see also Benedek, 1968, p. 444; Kestenberg, 1956, p. 463). Yet by now it is possible for writers on psychoanalysis and women, even those most sympathetic to the early Freudian perspective, wholly to ignore the existence of this key historic piece of work (see, for example, Fliegel, 1973; Nagera, 1975, 1976).

At the time of the appearance of her first book, Helene Deutsch was the founding President of the Training Institute of the Vienna Psychoanalytic Society (Siegfried Bernfeld was Vice-President, and Anna Freud was Secretary). All the patients who came for training in Vienna had to be interviewed and assessed by her, and already in 1925 she was on the way to becoming one of the most famous teachers in the history of Freud's movement. Wilhelm Reich, for example, was one of her ('wayward') protégés, and her students included the next generation of leading analysts, for instance Ernst Kris and Erik H. Erikson. Until she left for America in 1935, to become one of the first training analysts in Boston, she continued as Director of the Vienna Training Institute, and she had come to play an important role in Freud's immediate circle. Later, even following her official retirement in old age as a practising clinician, she remained a symbol of Freud's cause. (She outlived many of those she had taught, and she was still being interviewed and quoted in the late 1970s [Friday, 1977].) Her clinical studies and autobiography, as well as her two-volume *The Psychology of Women*—so encyclopaedic in scope as to invite later detractors—had made her one of the leading proponents of the Freudian outlook on femininity (Deutsch, 1965, 1967, 1973, 1944–45; see also Roazen, 1985).

In 1925, however, she was not the representative of an established school of thought but an innovator in a fresh and uncharted area of specialization. She had been well trained as a psychiatrist in both Vienna and Munich, and during the First World War (when her male colleagues were on the front) she went further within Viennese psychiatry than any woman had before her. In choosing officially to join the Vienna Psychoanalytic Society in 1918 and in undergoing a personal analysis with Freud in 1918–19 Helene Deutsch was taking leave of the conventional wisdom of her time. Freud was then an outsider to academic psychiatry throughout central Europe, and North American pupils had not yet begun to flock to him. She had been born in a small Polish town, a part of the Austro-Hungarian Empire, in 1884, and became an M.D. in 1913. But her own mother had been against higher education for her, thinking instead that a decent young girl should be married by the age of twenty. It is therefore only in historical perspective that Helene Deutsch's decision to become a follower of Freud can be appreciated.

The history of women has had its ahistorical elements. For although Simone de Beauvoir in *The Second Sex* (1961) valued the significance of Helene Deutsch's later ideas, some more recent political feminists, such as Susan Brownmiller, felt able to state that she was not 'a pioneer, but a traitor to her sex' (Gordon, 1978, p. 24; see also, for example, Brownmiller, 1975; Friedan, 1963; Greer, 1970; Reitz, 1979; Badinter, 1981). In contrast to women analysts like Karen Horney and Clara Thompson, for example, who came to revise Freudian ideas and emphasized the role of culture in giving meaning to psychological processes, Helene Deutsch remained convinced of the inevitability of fundamental differences between men and women. Yet inequalities between the sexes need not, Helene Deutsch thought, have anything to do with inferiorities.

For that matter, in historical context Helene Deutsch was herself a leading feminist. In 1914, for example, she had had the idea of founding a recuperative institution for young women aged fourteen to twenty; she wrote about the proposal in a letter to her husband Felix, whom she had married in 1912 and who later was Freud's personal physician for a time. As she described the clinical need for her undertaking, Helene Deutsch declaimed enthusiastically about treating such adolescent patients: 'Only a woman can understand and help them.' The upheaval of World War I made any such plans impossible. But one has to remember how relatively rare it was to be a career woman at that time.

Even as late as 1924, when she had publicly spoken for the first time about motherhood at an important meeting of analysts, a critically important former lover of hers, much older than herself, wrote with a reminder of their pre-war days together: 'I was very happy and proud about your success at the conference of psychoanalysis, just like in the old times and just as if you still belonged to me. Do you remember . . . your speech at that meeting in Vienna, about allowing women to study law? I was very proud of your success at that meeting then, and now I had the same feeling when reading the report of the conference.' Having defied her social background in becoming a doctor and left mainstream psychiatry in joining Freud, she was now able to discuss a subject that had been taken for granted within psychoanalytic thought.

Helene Deutsch deserves to be appreciated for having been a leading female psychiatrist. She regarded feminine psychology as a subject requiring as much attention as

that of men. Of all the early analysts, she more than any-
one else fleshed out the implications of Freud's ideas for
women. She remained a Freudian loyalist; but in as much
as his vision was a commanding one, she brought its
advantages to bear on the problem of femininity and in so
doing reduced its limitations. So, for example, in writing
about motherhood, she would come to emphasize, in keeping with Freud's tragic sense, the costs to a woman's erotic
life of having children (Deutsch, 1965). Yet whether she
was talking about motherhood as a normal developmental
phase, or the origins of the specific symptomatology of frigidity, Helene Deutsch was making original contributions.

Although feminist critiques of Freud have been abundant (see for example, Lasch, 1974; Millet, 1971; Gilman,
1971; see also Miller, 1976), some recent feminist
literature has adopted a different attitude towards
psychoanalysis; it has been seen not only as an accurate
account of the psychological oppression of women, but as a
source of insight into their potential liberation (Chodorow,
1978; Mitchell, 1974). In historical terms, Helene
Deutsch's career reminds us that throughout the twentieth
century women succeeded in going farther within the profession of psychoanalysis than in almost any field one can
think of. Senior analysts have sometimes reported that it
is easier to place referral patients with women than with
their male colleagues.

All innovators proceed at a certain peril; and with
hindsight many points they make may appear misdirected.
(Theodor Adorno once remarked about psychoanalysis as a
whole: 'Only the exaggerations are true.') In assessing the
Freudian perspective on women, and the turn Helene
Deutsch gave to psychoanalytic thinking, one needs understanding, open-mindedness, and tolerance. It is remarkable
how much of what she wrote in 1924 still bears reconsider-
ing today and is enduringly worthwhile.

It is a tribute to the vitality of Freud's ideas that so
much effort has been spent in challenging them. He had

insisted that people have bodies, and the psychosocial implications of this understanding are bound to be far-reaching. It is true that, for the individual, therapeutic suggestion can have an impact on its own. But even if it were possible to show that the Freudian revolution in ideas had, on balance, a negative influence, it has become so pervasively a part of our culture that some historical inquiry is necessary to account for the prevalence of his ideas.

One valuable, even if seemingly outdated, feature of Helene Deutsch's thinking needs emphasis. She was a broadly cultured woman who knew that however important female sexuality was, it ought not to be treated as exhausting all that was to be said about the feminine soul. Sex, no matter how broadly defined, is still, after all, only a part of life. As she wrote to her husband Felix with a sense of satisfaction on completing the manuscript of this book: 'It brings something new to this *terra incognita* in analysis—I believe, the first ray of light on the unappreciated female libido.[1] But what is more: I'm not making it the central part of existence. . . .'

After the completion of *Psychoanalysis of the Sexual Functions of Women,* Freud published three short but important papers of his own about female psychology. In 1933, concluding his last essay on femininity, Freud (1933a [1932]) apologized (in a civilized spirit similar to Helene Deutsch's 1924 letter to her husband) for the incomplete, fragmentary, and not always friendly-sounding nature of his views on women:

> But do not forget that I have only been describing women in so far as their nature is determined by their sexual function. It is true that that influence extends very far; but we do not overlook the fact that an individual woman may be a human being in other respects as well. If you want to know more about femininity, enquire from your own experiences of life, or turn to the poets, or wait until science can give you deeper and more coherent information.

NOTE

1. In 1905 Freud had maintained that 'libido is invariably and necessarily of a masculine nature, whether it occurs in men or in women and irrespectively of whether its object is a man or a woman'. In 1933 he modified this position by saying that 'there is only one libido, which serves both the masculine and the feminine sexual functions. To itself we cannot assign any sex. . . .' But then he went on to withdraw his apparent retraction: 'Nevertheless the juxtaposition "feminine libido" is without any justification' (Freud, 1905d; 1933a [1932]).

PSYCHOANALYSIS
OF THE SEXUAL FUNCTIONS
OF WOMEN

CHAPTER ONE

Introduction

Psychoanalysis of the Sexual Functions of Women was written during 1923–24, while Helene Deutsch was separated from her husband Felix. She had gone to Berlin, accompanied by her six-year-old son, for a second analysis with Karl Abraham, who had pioneered in the subject of female psychology; she also wanted to learn about the way in which the Berlin Psychoanalytic Institute was set up, thinking that it would help her to organize the Vienna training facilities she was to head. During the latter half of her stay away from Vienna, the boy was left in the charge of Felix, who was then beginning to make innovations in the area of psychosomatic medicine. The surge of medical interest in the interaction of the mind and the body, which reached its height after World War II, has now subsided, but at the time Helene Deutsch was writing psychological and somatic phenomena were conventionally far more compartmentalized than today.

Throughout most of the book she confined herself to theoretical concepts. After Freud first contracted cancer in 1923, he never published another case history; the spectre of his own death made him more speculative. Helene Deutsch's book was written in the shadow of Freud's illness. In contrast to almost all her other writings, clinical illustrations (except for the last chapter) are left out. She was explicitly addressing herself to a professional audience. But by now psychoanalytic thinking has become sufficiently widely known for her work to be understood by the educated public.

The following considerations are based on observations made over many years. This material is intended to give a psychological dimension to knowledge of the processes summed up under the general term of 'sexual life of women'.

To avoid the criticism of one-sidedness, let it be stated at the outset that these observations are restricted to the psychological field; they take somatic phenomena into account only insofar as they represent the point of departure of psychical reactions or alternatively are made use of as the physical expression of mental processes.

The clinical material on which these theoretical conclusions are based will be referred to practically not at all here; that material is reserved for a subsequent fuller publication, which will be intended to make the analytic findings accessible to non-analysts also. This short work assumes a thorough knowledge of psychoanalysis. Some chapters have already been presented to a psychoanalytic audience ('Psychology of the reproductive functions' at the Eighth International Psycho-analytic Congress at Salzburg, Easter, 1924; 'Psychology of the menopause', at the First German Conference for Psycho-analysis, Salzburg, October, 1924).

Previous analytic contributions to the psychological understanding of women will be taken into account and mentioned here. All other psychological findings, insofar as they are based on psychology of the conscious, will not be referred to here, for it is the purpose of this book to explain what was bound to remain mysterious to the psychology of the conscious because it was inaccessible to its methods.

But even in depth psychology understanding of mental processes in women has lagged behind that of the same processes in men. In particular, little analytic attention has been paid to the generative processes, though these form the centre point of the mental life of the sexually mature woman. Kant's saying that woman does not betray her secret still applies. The hidden contents of the male mind have obviously been more accessible to the male because of the closer kinship.

All the new insights into the mental life of woman in her relations to the reproductive function that will be reported here were gained with the aid of the analytic method.

We shall confine ourselves here to communicating findings connected with woman's psychological relations to the physiological processes of sexual life.

In our method of working it has often been from the pathological that we have gained understanding of the normal, and in the same way for the purpose of facilitating understanding we shall refer to the pathological when it presents itself as a caricature of certain constellations in the normal. Also, in the processes with which we are concerned here, concomitant psychical phenomena occur, which, though one would not describe them as normal in the physiological sense, should no longer be classified as morbid because of their regular and typical appearance in our cultural conditions.

The problems to be discussed in this book refer to the sexual life of woman throughout the duration of her sexual maturity, i.e., from the beginning of puberty onwards. Special attention will be paid to the psychical reactions to the various acts of the reproductive function.

CHAPTER TWO

Female infantile sexuality

Helene Deutsch naturally began with an account of early childhood, regarded by Freud as the prime source of adult character. Psychoanalysis stressed the fundamental reality of human infantile helplessness. These early stages of life had not yet been studied on the basis of direct observations, but reconstructed from the dreams, memories, symptoms, and fantasies of analytic patients. It would be mistaken to believe, however, that more recent approaches have necessarily rejected his view of the importance of these earliest years.

It is now thought by some—for example, by students of gender identity—that the core convictions 'I am a boy' or 'I am a girl' are fixed by the age of two or three (see, for example, Money & Ehrhardt, 1973). Parental hopes and expectations have a powerful impact on how children are reared. Furthermore, genetic differences and sexual hormones already begin to play a part pre-natally, five or six weeks after a child has been conceived.

It is well known that Freud proclaimed that 'anatomy is destiny', but classical psychoanalysis was—by some current standards—relatively hopeful about how long it was before personality is finally formed. The height of the Oedipus complex (the most intense feelings towards father and mother) takes place, in Freud's view, between the ages of five and six. Freud's theories, based on his clinical experience, reflect the importance of conflict; and although he did not sufficiently emphasize what many would now see as important features of early sexual organization, he was at the same time highlighting possibilities for change. Puberty was a second chance for a reorganization of human drives. Freud may at times have overemphasized the role of early development in character formation, but Helene Deutsch certainly wanted to talk about other stages of life as well. In addition to writing on adolescence, she also considered the strengths and problems associated with motherhood.

She relies on Freud's model of childhood development. Even if the terms 'oral', 'anal', and 'phallic' seem to some to have a dated ring today, it must be remembered that they refer to the instinctual organization and not to the rest of the personality. In 1950 Erik H. Erikson extended earlier formulations through ego-oriented concepts such as 'trust', 'autonomy', and 'initiative'. These are now familiar and widely accepted notions (Erikson, 1963; Roazen, 1976). But it was the early formulation of instinctual stages linked to erotogenic zones that made its greatest impact and became popularized—for instance in the child-rearing handbooks of Dr Spock.

Helene Deutsch's 1925 audience was well-versed in a specialized vocabulary, and when she writes about 'sadism' she is taking for granted a professional understanding that she referred to no specially cruel impulse alone, but rather to a drive to overcome and master. By genital sadism, she tells us later (see chapter four), she simply means 'an active-libidinal taking possession of the object', although this drive might take on a regressively hostile or destructive aim. The language of early psychoanalysis tended to be stylized.

The emphasis on the psychological significance of the presence or absence of the penis was in the mid-1920s considered by analysts to be basic to any discussion of femininity. It seems to the present writer that the early Freudians over-did the literal meaning of the anatomical differences between the sexes, and that Freud failed to understand how much certain organs of the body could be used to symbolize powerful or weak social roles. 'Feminine castration anxiety' was a technical correlative of what became widely known as penis envy; it was a term that seemed to explain in part how it could come about that women were disparaged, resentful, or disappointed. Helene Deutsch, like so many of her colleagues, concentrated in her theories on apparently innate developmental problems. Later writers, such as Erich Fromm (1963), would instead look for the cultural bases of what they regarded as psychological prejudices.

Karen Horney was a leading figure in challenging Freud's theories of women; and in their later works she and Helene Deutsch would pause to tangle with each other (see, for example, Horney, 1973, pp. 148, 157n, 161n, 214–18, 222–223, 231; Deutsch, 1944, pp. 231, 278. See also Garrison, 1981; Quinn, 1987; Rubins, 1978). In her extensive review article of *Psychoanalysis of the Sexual Functions of Women,* however, Karen Horney (1926) might have had reservations about some features of this work; but she thought that it was

of the greatest value that an undertaking like the subjection of the whole range of female sexual functioning to psychoanalytic consideration should be attempted at all. . . . One cannot do justice to a country-side if one only travels along its main thorough-fares, and in the same way this review which has to keep strictly to the main ideas cannot do justice to the real wealth of observation and thought that this work contains. [pp. 92, 100]

Although their ideas subsequently went in different directions, and helped fuel an important controversy over female psychology that has preoccupied many, it would be mistaken to date back all their later disagreements to the mid-1920s. (Melanie Klein, an analyst who differed from Freud's views on women, relied at various points on *Psychoanalysis of the Sexual Functions of Women*.) In contrast to the way in which Helene Deutsch always couched her modifications of Freud in tactful language, Karen Horney went on to develop her own independent system of thought; but by the 1940s Helene Deutsch (1944, pp. 194, 226, 230, 238) had her own qualifications and reservations to make, for instance in connection with penis envy. (See also Webster, 1985, p. 562.)

It is worth remembering that at the time Helene Deutsch was writing in 1924, Karen Horney (1973, pp. 37–53) had recently proposed that a girl's identification with her father was an explanation for a neurotic lack of femininity. Unlike Karen Horney, from the outset of her work on female psychology Helene Deutsch was trying to include an intimate tie with a woman's father as a normal source of personality growth, an enhancement of the ego.

This original point of Helene Deutsch's, part of the way she used the theory of bisexuality, is expressed throughout her work in terms of the libido theory, with which by no means everyone agrees today. She shares Freud's view that as compensation for the acceptance of 'castration' the young girl identifies with her mother in the yearning for a child. An essential component of Freud's outlook had been the price we pay for things; for him, developmental progress also entails and is connected with regressive tendencies, and Helene Deutsch's next chapter addresses the issue of the 'masculinity complex'.

A word is in order about her emphasis on guilt associated with clitoral masturbation. Helene Deutsch had for years been a hard-working therapist but had seldom clinically encountered stories of vaginal masturbation. To the extent that she sought therapeutically to encourage female patients to engage in heterosexual relationships, clitoral masturbation was implicitly being discouraged by considering it, as Freud did, a 'masculine' trait in women. Currently, the pendulum has swung in an opposite direction, so that female patients are often actively encouraged, though not by most psychoanalysts themselves, to explore their own bodies.

It has always been an open question, however, where to draw the line between too much and too little. Freud's own 1912 uncertainties about the consequences of masturbation seem reasonably level-headed today. He was, of course, then thinking in terms of male psychology, and the legendary effect of masturbation in reducing potency. (Perhaps only in North America, which has long popularly defined manliness in terms of cowboyism, does masturbation in youths still evoke a dread of homosexuality.) Freud (1912f) sounds like a dry sceptic when he writes about men:

Some diminution of male potency and of the brutal aggressiveness involved in it is much to the purpose from the point of view of civilization. It facilitates the practice by civilized men of the virtues of sexual moderation and trustworthiness that are incumbent on them. Virtue accompanied by full potency is usually felt as a hard task.

Helene Deutsch, like Freud, was working within a somewhat abstract and ascetic vein of thought. Yet no matter how readily contemporary sex therapists might discard individual parts of Freud's system of thought, few would deny the commanding stature of the edifice he bequeathed to history.

The foundation stone of the science of psychoanalysis was the discovery that sexual life begins in earliest infancy. Sexual development is eventually completed at puberty, when the infantile sexual drives are combined in the interests of the function of reproduction.

For the better understanding of the processes to be discussed here it seems appropriate to begin by mentioning some psychoanalytic findings about the early period of sexual life in women. Our starting-point will be the phase before the latency period, when the difference between male and female first expresses itself in the infantile sexual organization.

We know that the definitive separation of the sexes comes about only with the beginning of the reproductive function (or the readiness for it), but that from earliest infancy distinctive features appear in boys and girls. The conclusion of the stage of infantile sexual organization takes place under the aegis of a very far-reaching differentiation.

At the earliest level of organization the development of the female libido is identical with that of the male. The first two pre-genital phases, the oral and the anal-sadistic, are completely similar in both sexes, both in instinctual trends and in cathexis of the erogenous zones. Similarly, the composition of the sexual trends as a result of the object-choice made in earliest infancy is the same in both sexes. In both it provides the content of the Oedipus complex, which in the case of the boy forms around the choice of the mother as love object, and that of the father in the case of the girl. In both sexes this constellation involves hostility and rivalry towards the parent of the same sex. Psychoanalysis has shown us the significance of this infantile attitude and revealed its role both in the final shaping of normal love life and in neurotic illnesses.

Infantile sexuality ends, as Freud (1923e) has shown us, in the third, or 'phallic' phase, in which the destiny of the Oedipus constellation is decided.

The introduction of the 'phallic' phase into the development of the libido also explained to us a great deal about the development of the feminine libido and for the first time made the subsequent development of the latter completely clear to us. For a full understanding of the pubertal psychology that concerns us here we must start from the processes in the 'phallic' phase.

We know that in her unconscious sadistically conceived fantasies of coitus in the anal-sadistic phase the little girl (just like the boy) identifies now with the father, now with the mother. Identification with the father involves sadistic ideas, while identification with the mother implies passive-anal suffering. The sadistic component of these fantasies assumes possession of the active penis; the mother's passive role corresponds to the fantasy of the anal child.

In the phallic phase the passive tendencies are suppressed, just as they are in the case of the boy; the girl's interest is centred on the clitoris, which for her has the significance of the penis. Identification with the father is continued in relation to the clitoris and—as in the active sadistic tendencies of the previous phase—is expressed in the 'male' trends of that organ. In the girl, as in the boy, masturbatory activity in the service of the Oedipus complex is centred on the genitals. Until the discovery of the opposite, the clitoris is regarded as an organ of absolutely sterling value cathected with large quantities of pleasure.

Acceptance of the sad discovery of the lack of a penis is accompanied by resistances. The small girl tries to console herself with hope for the future; the fact of the absence of the penis is often felt to be an affliction affecting her only, and in fantasies of revenge responsibility is attributed sometimes to the mother, sometimes to the father; and, finally, the individual's own masturbation and Oedipus fantasies are regarded as the cause of the grievous loss. The discovered and accepted lack of the penis is regularly regarded as the infliction of a punishment.

Freud (1924d) has shown us how the downfall of the boy's Oedipus complex takes place at the hands of the castration threat; the boy sacrifices the libidinal cathexes related to the parents in order to remain in narcissistic possession of the penis. 'The object cathexes are given up and are replaced by identification—paternal or parental authority introjected into the ego there forms the nucleus of the superego' (Freud, 1924d).

It is different in the case of the girl, who finally accepts castration as an accomplished fact. 'With the elimination of the fear of castration a powerful motive for the erection of the superego and the demolition of the infantile organization is lacking.'

In the case of the girl these processes assume a more complicated form. We have seen that the assumed possession of the penis in the form of the actively directed clitoris represented a continuation of the sadistic tendencies of the previous level of development and went hand in hand with an identification with the father. With the giving up of the clitoris identification with the father has to be given up too. The girl finds an explanation for her lack of a penis, i.e., for the castration she has suffered, in the masturbatory activity which for the first time is associated with intense guilt feelings. This guilt is not identical with the fear of castration of the boy who is faced with this punishment if he does not give up the reason for the guilt, but is a threat and a warning about future sinful tendencies that in the girl's case, as in the boy's, are rooted in the Oedipus complex. Thus guilt feeling in the case of the girl arises in this phase after she believes she has discovered that masturbation involves a punishment as severe as castration.

Thus in the girl's case, as in the boy's, the castration complex provides an impulse to the formation of the superego. But as the punishment has already been suffered, this is more weakly developed, as Freud tells us, and the 'downfall of the Oedipus complex' comes about only by indirect routes. We have seen that identification with the father had to be given up with the first renunciation of the clitoris. What happens to the identification is this. In the first place it is elevated to a higher plane by being desexualized and set up in the superego. The narcissistic wound involved in the penis loss is wiped out by an enhancement of the ego on the issues of: 'Though I do not possess what father possesses, I am like him all the same.' Thus in the case of the female the formation of the superego also takes place by means of an introjection of the father. Secondly, with renunciation of possession of the penis the narcissistic relationship to the father moves to the higher level of object-libido. At this phase the sway of the girl's superego turns out to be weaker than the libidinal forces. The abandonment of the clitoris and the narcissistic wound associated with that have mobilized the regressive mechanisms, and wounded narcissism seeks compensation. With the giving up of the active organ the passive-anal components of the previous phase are regressively cathected, and the identification with the mother associated with that and the wish for the 'anal child' as compensation for the loss of the penis are renewed. In the girl's wishful fantasies the father becomes what he is to the mother, i.e., a sex object. In the previous phase, faeces had already been given the meaning of 'child', and after giving up the clitoris as penis in the 'phallic' phase the old wish is cathected with new quantities not in the sense of a progression from the clitoris to the vagina, which remains undiscovered for a long time yet, but in the sense of a regression to the anal level. Thus the girl's last stage of infantile development is divided into two phases: first, the phallic phase, in which the clitoris is cathected with large quantities of libido and equated in value with the penis, while its tendencies are completely male and are rooted in identification with the father.

In the second phase, after the 'discovery' of castration as an accomplished fact, clitoral sexuality is given up, and a regressive activation of passive-anal trends and of the wish for an 'anal child' takes place in an identification with the mother. It can be said that in the case of the girl, unlike that of the boy, the 'phallic' phase is connected with a first appearance of passivity that prefigures the processes of puberty.

In the girl the infantile organization comes to an end only in this passively oriented phase; only now does the downfall of the girl's Oedipus complex take place.

Freud assumes that 'the Oedipus complex is abandoned because the child's wish is never fulfilled'. To that the following can be added. The superego that has been formed in the meantime has by now set up the incest ban, and the resulting guilt feelings end by forcing the girl to give up her rivalry with the mother. Identification with the mother now moves to a higher phase of superego formation and gives its specific character to the female ego-ideal. This is idealized maternity and a definite sexual morality and sexual inhibition characteristic of the moral woman that originates from this ego ideal formation. When this ego-ideal formation from the introjection of the mother fails, the latter remains an 'inferior sex object', and identification with her in this contest contributes to the formation of the 'whore complex' in the female. The formation of the ego-ideal can take place in various ways. Either identification with the father predominates, in which case the woman tends to sublimation on male lines, or identification with the mother prevails, in which case the ego-ideal is a Madonna-like maternity. But both forms can be connected in a quite special way, when the paternal ideal is continued in the product of her female sublimation, the child.

In the 'phallic' phase the discovery of the loss of the penis was followed by guilt feelings. The final phase of the 'anal child' is similarly associated with strong guilt feelings. Cases can occasionally be observed in which psychogenic sterility is conditioned by the guilt feelings of this phase. As the valuation of the penis—after its loss by castration—was carried over to the child, the girl in her unconscious feels herself obliged also to renounce the child in a kind of renewed castration. She believes she must give up hope of a child as she once gave up hope of a penis.

Infantile sexual organization comes to an end in the process described above in about the fifth year of life and is succeeded by the latency period. Observation has shown us that the 'latency' of this period is only relative. Residues of previous developments manifest themselves in it, continuing various components of these developments and putting special emphasis on them. At the same time the foundations for the psychological changes of puberty are gradually laid.

It was only the discovery of the phallic level of organization in the development of the libido that enabled us completely to explain the origin and significance of the 'masculinity complex'.

CHAPTER THREE

The masculinity complex in women

The use of the term 'complex', first introduced into the psychoanalytic vocabulary by Carl G. Jung, can be elucidated by the concept of 'conflict'. Helene Deutsch wanted to treat the masculinity complex in women as a normal part of personality development. In her opening remarks in this chapter, she mentions two sources of femininity in men: (1) the persistence of earlier 'passive' trends, and (2) an identification with the mother. As late as a case history published in 1918, Freud (1918b [1914], p. 27) had held that the little boy's earliest, most intimate attachment was to his father. Freud, particularly in the 1920s, had been specific in suggesting that the Oedipus complex of the boy could reverse the so-called positive feelings of attachment to the parent of the opposite sex and rivalry towards the parent of the same sex.

Freud understood the mother as an object of sexual desire and a source of sensual pleasure. But he did not emphasize the mother's protective functions or her nurturing role, and he did not even mention the mother as a

17

figure on whom the child at an early age establishes a legitimate dependency. By and large Freud took for granted the nurturing functions of a mother. He did not exclude the mother's part in the psychopathology of male patients; but he saw her mainly as either a seductress into an oedipal situation or the source of adult homosexual conflicts.

Helene Deutsch was not the only analyst at the time who was beginning to emphasize the relatively neglected role of the mother. Otto Rank (1929), Georg Groddeck (1961), and Sandor Ferenczi (1938) were all coming to similar conclusions, although they each did so in their own characteristic ways. (Rank and Ferenczi [1956], for example, were interested in new approaches to therapeutic technique.) Helene Deutsch was the one analyst, however, to look on motherhood primarily from the perspective of female psychology.

Before getting to her more general thesis about the significance of female reproductive capacities, Helene Deutsch made an effort to demonstrate the exceptionally strong part played by bisexual trends in the psychology of women. She was of course writing at a time when women were more or less restricted to life with their families, when it was unusual to feel blocked from pursuing professional goals. She did not, as she would in 1944 (Deutsch, 1944, p. 147), connect her psychological theories to the greater social premium on masculine qualities, which was relevant to her proposition that 'the "masculinity complex" in women plays a much more dominant role than the "femininity complex" in man. . . .' Instead, she agreed with Freud's starting point that a little girl feels psychologically that her anatomy is a handicap, and she accepted the clinical evidence of Karl Abraham and Karen Horney that female development entails other disadvantages.

In contrast to Karen Horney, who saw in a woman's identification with her father the rejection of a feminine

role, Helene Deutsch insisted that such a bond to a
father need not be neurotic. In effect she was using bio-
logical-sounding theory for purposes of female emancipation. At the conclusion of her own analysis with
Freud he had encouraged her to 'stay on the road of
identification' with her father, a prominent lawyer.
Instead of simply reducing her positive relationship to
her father to penis envy, Freud saw it as the basis for
her successful career as a woman. However much
Freud's theories might reflect the social patterns of his
time, in practice he was remarkably broad-minded. As
another female analyst, also a former patient of Freud's,
wrote in 1934 protesting against his mature views on
femininity: 'It is not a credible view of women. . . . Freud
himself has not always looked at women thus' (Riviere,
1934, p. 336).

The concept of penis envy now seems to some,
especially non-analysts, an outgrowth of the patriarchal
bias Freud shared with his social order. Women's complaints of deprivation, conscious and unconscious, as well
as the consequent desire for revenge, were realistic signs
of social injustice. Yet in the context of the history of
psychoanalytic theory, the notion of penis envy was
designed to co-ordinate female psychology with that of
men.

Freud had long thought that castration anxiety, an
irrational basis for contempt and derision of women,
was a crucial aspect of unconscious male thinking.
According to Freud's 1925 theory of normal human
development, whereas in men the Oedipus complex was
overcome ('dissolved') by the threat of castration, in
women the impact of the anatomical absence of a male
organ preceded and prepared for the creation of an
Oedipus complex. Although in one sense the idea of
unconscious penis envy may have seemed to lower women's status, especially as Freud insufficiently emphasized male jealousy (or fear) of a woman's reproductive

capacities, his theory was now attempting to put female development on an equal conceptual footing with that of men.

In my view this early generation of analytic thinkers made too much of the cognitive perception of the differences between the sexes. Yet knowledge and enlightenment were at the same time viewed as powerful therapeutic tools. It was believed that neurosis could be prophylactically alleviated thanks to superior childhood sex education; this conviction is still relevant to much contemporary thought about sexual learning (Gagnon, 1965). Within psychoanalysis it would take someone like Wilhelm Reich (1970; see, for example, Roazen, 1990, pp. 126–128, 209–212) to dare to propose that what was necessary was a fundamental re-arrangement of Western middle-class family life.

P sychoanalytic experience forces us more and more to the conclusion that the 'masculinity complex' in women is a permanent component of their psychical structure and that it is only under definite conditions that its presence leads to neurotic phenomena. Otherwise it occurs in normal reaction formations, sublimations, character formations and other forms. This fact seems to be explained by the assumption of the bisexual constitution of the human species, and the 'masculinity' that appears in feminine mental life would thus be merely a residue of a past state of development that had not been completely overcome. The mental life of men is also permeated with reminiscences of phases of development that, because of their nature, which conflicts with 'masculinity', represents the 'feminine' component in masculine mental life. In these cases we are always confronted with the persistence of 'passive' trends from phases in which, though masculinity and femininity were not yet present, the preliminary stages of this polarity were already prefigured in the 'active' and the 'passive'.

We regard the identification of the mother that arises out of the Oedipus complex and disappears in the normal course of development as a second source of feminine trends in the male. This identification plays an important part in the origin of the neuroses and the perversions.

If these conclusions bear witness to the presence of bisexual elements in the male, the 'masculinity complex' in woman plays a much more dominant role than the 'femininity complex' in man, so that genetically a different meaning must be ascribed to it.

The assumption that the 'masculinity complex' was a reaction to the handicap suffered by the small girl as a result of the sad fact of lacking a penis became the foundation-stone of psychoanalytic theory in the matter. 'Anatomy is destiny', said Freud, varying a phrase of Napoleon's. The identity of this complex with the castration or penis envy complex was thus established. Since Abraham's (1922) pioneering work, the 'masculinity complex' has been regarded as an expression of the narcissistic wound of lacking the penis. In the clinical and descriptive sense there is nothing to add to Abraham's far-reaching work; it contains everything that we know at present about this constellation.

But the view that the masculinity complex is to be attributed only to the fact of anatomical handicap seems to ascribe full importance to only one motive and to neglect others that are perhaps just as important.

K. Horney's (1924) paper accords with the need to find other explanations for the formation of this complex, and she succeeds in demonstrating other aetiological factors based on clinical material.

She assumes that in addition to the narcissistic wound of anatomical deficiency there are other disadvantageous factors that must be taken into account, above all the impossibility of satisfying certain partial drives that are of importance in the pregenital phases. Possession of the male organ implies an important role for urinary erotism, exhibitionism, and better opportunities for the unpenalized practice of masturbation.

In the paper referred to Horney puts forward the proposition that identification with the parent of the opposite sex represents the point of departure for the development of the female castration complex. Through identification with the father the feminine role is declined, and the wish for the penis associated with this from which the castration complex derives accords with this. The failure of the Oedipus complex is regarded as explaining the origin of the identification. Thus the failure of female wishes is a secondary factor in the creation of the castration complex, and it is not the castration complex that is a primary factor in hindering female development.

This contribution by Horney has turned out to be important for the understanding of the female castration complex and supplements Abraham's pioneering work. Extensive experience enables me fully to confirm the assumption that identification with the father plays a central role in the formation of the masculinity complex. Also, failure of the Oedipus complex as a reason for regression is given the importance that is well known to us elsewhere, without, however, fully explaining the regularity of these analytic findings in normal psychical life.

This regularity points to a biological cause existing in the process of development, and the pathological phenomena would correspond to regressive processes, quantitative reinforcements, fixations, etc., just as we are used to observing in the development of other morbid processes.

Study of the phallic phase seems to show that the dispositional factors for the formation of the masculinity complex can be sought in that phase, and that all its normal and pathological expressions can be brought under the heading of phallic complex.

The never-overcome disappointment at the genital loss and the reaction associated with it are not only to be sought in the 'narcissistic wound' of physical inferiority. They are closely connected with instinctual development and are bound up with constitutional factors.

The sadistic trends of the pre-genital phase are raised to a higher level in the phallic phase, i.e., they no longer aim at the destruction of the object but appear under the aegis of 'activity', i.e., of aggression without destruction. The passive trends of the previous phase undergo repression or are given up with the following motivation: the possession of faeces as a narcissistic value is devalued both externally and internally—externally by reactions of disgust on the part of the educational environment, internally through the loss factor, the recurrent shedding process. This devaluation leads the narcissistic libido of both sexes to the discovery of a new source in the individual's own body. In the phallic phase the genital organ becomes the centre of narcissistic libido just as the faeces were in the previous phase. By this biogenetically prefigured path the pregenital phase ends with devaluation of the faeces, and narcissistic over-valuation passes to the penis.

Just as the anus previously put itself at the disposal of passive tendencies, so does the penis now do the same for active ones, though its narcissistic value also brings it residues of anal tendencies.

The passive tendencies of the previous phase are given up with the devaluation of the product, and with it identification with the mother.

We have already seen that for boy and girl alike the phallic phase is under the aegis of identification with the father. Pathology tells us that in the boy identification with the mother goes hand in hand with the castration wish and with clinging to the anal components of the libido. Normally the anal trends in the male, which should be abandoned at this stage, become an important source of sublimation. The product of work output as a faeces–child equivalent derives from this, and in this way the feminine instinctual components of the male are made use of. We have already discussed the destiny of anal trends in the female.

At all events, in the cathexis of the genitals with narcissistic libido on the one hand and sadistic-active tendencies on the other, the girl's clitoris is equated in value with the boy's penis. The libido under the aegis of identification with the father assumes the presence of an active organ, just as sadism assumes that of physical muscles. Possession of the active genital organ represents a biological necessity for this phallic phase of development. For the boy this phase represents a step forward in the direction of his future development towards sexual maturity; to the girl it represents the final act of her bisexual constitution, the crossroads at which differentiation between male and female appears for the first time in her infantile sexual organization.

The small girl has no doubt about the full value of the clitoris, which functions as the male organ; she feels herself in possession of the organ that her actual libidinal trends demand. The intensive pressure of the clitoris, the lurking suspicion of its absence, the direction of attention to the pleasure-cathected zone, the inner necessity of the organ itself, lead to investigation, comparison, to the secondary discovery of the difference and the formation of the castration complex.

Thus the masculinity complex is built up on a biogenetically conditioned masculine phase in which identification with the father must be regarded as a progressive, not a regressive, process. At this phase the clitoris has the value of the real penis, and only by the giving up of that valuation does it lead to the formation of the castration complex.

With the shift of narcissistic libido to the genitals the latter are affected by the fear of loss for which there was a real foundation in the previous phase. For, as we showed above, it was the loss factor that provided the impulse for the creation of the new erogenous zone. The child's whole attention is now concentrated in two directions: on the organ itself and on the reaction of the environment. It must be emphasized that before the discovery of the lack of the penis, that is, before the formation of the reactive castration complex, the small girl develops the same anxiety about the clitoris that the small boy develops about the penis. Analytic experience makes us very familiar with the girl's castration anxiety, which is completely identical with that of the boy and assumes the existence of that organ. The genesis of that anxiety is to be sought in the stage of development preceding the discovery of the anatomical difference. In expectation of punishment for masturbation the child is on the alert for clues to the attitude of the environment, and everything suitable for that purpose is interpreted as a castration threat. The latter does not have to be directly staged to be felt as such by the child.

As a result of concentration of the interest on the genitals and observation of their environment, children, boys and girls alike, discover the genital difference. This discovery is now worked up on a basis of sexual differentiation. The boy gives up the pleasure function in order to retain anatomical possession. In the girl the process is different: above all, because of the lack of the organ, the phallic phase, and with it identification with the father, i.e., the masculinity constellation, has to be abandoned. Before this happens, there is a reaction-formation to the narcissistic wound of the newly made discovery. It is interesting to note that discovery of the sexual difference produces a traumatic reaction only when it takes place in the phallic phase of development. Observations made before this phase, even though the difference is visually perceived, are not made use of affectively and acquire their far-reaching significance only subsequently in the phallic phase.[1]

In special conditions of development fixation in the phallic stage can take place, with the result that the girl may end her infantile genital organization at the same stage of development as the boy.

In this case the castration complex as a reaction to the narcissistic wound cannot take place in the usual fashion, for the girl clings to the assumption of real possession of the penis, does not accept the sexual difference, and continues to identify with the father. She forms a superego of the male type, and in object-relations she becomes homosexual or chooses a heterosexual relationship in which she can retain the male role.

Normally identification with the father is given up with the discovery of the lack of a penis, and the next phase of the struggle about the lost organ, the tendency to persist with identification of the father, reactions to the lack of the organ, attempts to find consolation and explanation, the assumption that punishment has been inflicted, penis envy, desire for revenge, etc., forms the nucleus of the castration complex, which, even when suitably overcome, always leaves traces in the unconscious.

The ending of this struggle is equivalent to the giving up of the phallic organization. Any abnormal expression of this complex thus means a regression of the libido to the phallic phase. Thus certain forms of character formation in women are to be regarded as the offspring of this phase.

Abraham (1922) distinguished two types as 'forms of expression of the female castration complex', depending on the pattern of reaction; he notes a wishful and a vengeful type. On the basis of what we have said above we can add a third type, which, as we mentioned above, has never completely abandoned identification with the father, clings to real possession of the penis, and compromises between reality and the pleasure principle by denying lack of the penis. The female genitals remain permanently undiscovered (frigidity), the clitoris retains its fully satisfying sexual role, and the penis is never exchanged for the desire for a child. This type tends to homosexual object-choice, never attains the female attitude to the male, and is very masculine in its sublimatory trends. This is the pure 'masculinity complex', in which the reactive formations of the castration complex remain in the background.

Two types occur as a result of reaction-formations to the perceived castration:

1. The castration is regarded as a punishment, and characteristic inferiority feelings arise, originating partly from the sense of physical handicap and partly from guilt feeling;

2. The narcissistic wound is felt to be an injustice suffered, and intensive tendencies to exact revenge exist in relation to the world of objects (Abraham's vengeful type). The central feature is penis envy, and it is to be noted in this connection that this envy is above all directed towards the brother (it was prefigured in the sibling relationship). In later life it frequently expresses itself in competitive and emulative attitudes. Active castration wishes in relation to the father are more libidinal in nature in relation to the object and serve the tendencies to exact revenge, for unfulfilled libidinal demands. In contrast to this, the active castration wish in relation to the brother is rooted in the purely narcissistic wound of lacking the penis. It will always appear in analysis that the vengeful type has shown stronger sadistic impulses in the pregenital phase and has taken these over into the active trends of the phallic organization.

Thus in the phallic phase we have acquainted ourselves with a level of development of the libido in which the bisexual constitution of women reaches its high point but also its conclusion.

We have already discussed how identification with the mother then develops.

The final phase of infantile organization represented progress towards the 'female attitude' but is nevertheless a regression from the point of view of libido development (see above). This regressive feature is characteristic of 'femininity' and enables us to understand why it is that the equation of feminine and infantile appears so frequently in various psychical constellations.[2]

NOTES

1. At the age of eighteen months a girl noticed the sexual difference on the ocasion of the birth of her brother without reactions of any kind. The little boy's early death gave her no subsequent opportunity to revive the impressions made, the genesis of her castration complex belonged to a much later period of her childhood, and it was only then that the impression gained on that early occasion had an effect.
2. Dr W. Reich has told me that he too has been struck in his analyses by this regressive tendency in the normal development of the female libido.

CHAPTER FOUR

Differentiation between male and female in the reproductive period

This short section of her book was designed as a transition to an original contribution with which Helene Deutsch was more at home. In a paper first presented in 1924 (Deutsch, 1948a), she had begun to develop her ideas about the significance of the functions of reproduction for feminine psychology. (This paper, to her chagrin, was never cited by Freud, although she mentioned it at the outset of *Psycho-Analysis of the Sexual Functions of Women*; the issue of priorities was terribly important to Freud and the early analysts—see, for example, Roazen, 1975, p. 474; Roazen, 1969.)

She takes for granted a conceptual contrast between passivity as a feminine quality and activity as a masculine one. This continues to perplex some who think about sexual distinctions and who point out that feminine sexual functioning involves a high degree of activity, just as any man must be able to tolerate passive waiting. But this was not what Helene Deutsch meant: she was treating the issue within the context of bisexu-

ality. This kind of misunderstanding might have
been avoided if Helene Deutsch had spoken of role
'receptivity' rather than 'passivity'.

But Helene Deutsch tended, like Freud, to link masochism with feminine trends in the organism and
sadism with masculine ones (see for example, Blum,
1976; Chasseguet-Smirgel, 1976; Galenson, 1976). In
doing so she may have discounted the everyday over-
tones to the specialized vocabulary she was using. One
ought not to suppose that she was advocating one or the
other for either sex. Analysts had regularly encountered
both men and women whose unconscious self-infliction
of suffering was one of the main objects of psychoanalytic treatment. For women, masochism might mean
sexual inhibition, or a passion for men who mistreat
them; and in a 1930 paper Helene Deutsch (1948a)
sought to understand more about feminine masochism
and its relation to frigidity.

It can be argued that the upshot of Helene Deutsch's
work was to isolate and combat the woman's 'greater
disposition' to neurosis that she talks about here. In
Freud's view, neurosis was a sign of civilization (and an
Oedipus complex an achievement). With all the so-called
advances since 1925, it is still true that abundant evidence supports the notion that women suffer from mental problems more than do men; they pay more visits to
doctors, take up more places in hospitals, and use pills
more frequently (Chesler, 1972). Freud's conviction,
which Helene Deutsch was elaborating, was that the differentiation between the sexes imposes a much greater
burden on the female. Women were, in terms of this theory, more complicated and therefore more interesting.
Although today many would place greater emphasis on
the role of culture in bringing about the unhappy state
of affairs of women's greater disposition to neurosis, the
brute fact of the matter is that, despite all the social
changes since 1925, the clinical situation remains very
much the same.

To the extent that motherhood, according to Helene Deutsch, plays a special role in female development, femininity was not just a series of lacks; granted all the elements of disappointments and defeats in being a woman, she was not just isolating these deprivations but trying to put them into a larger, more positive framework. To a woman the coital act itself becomes only a part of a much broader process. In keeping with the emphasis within early psychoanalysis on traumatic aspects of psychological development, Helene Deutsch sought to pin-point those crises that were specifically female. If Freud had thought that women were more mysterious than men, this was part of his belief that their particular problems evoked unique capacities. Helene Deutsch, for example, in writing about menstrual periods as repetitions of adolescent difficulties, was aware (like other members of her social class) of Goethe's maxim that genius is the capacity for having repeated puberties.

We have already noted that different features appear in boys and girls in earliest infancy and that a big advance in differentiation between the sexes takes place in the phallic phase. But we must emphasize that the definitive separation of the sexes into male and female (in the psychological sense) becomes a fact only at puberty, that is, with the establishment of the reproductive function—or with the readiness for it. So we shall now concern ourselves with the psychology of woman in those aspects of life in which she is completely female, biologically and psychologically divergent from man.

It is only with the advent of the reproductive period that the identification of feminine with passive and masculine with active attains full validity, also implying a link between femininity and masochism and between masculinity and sadism, not only in the functional sense but also in that of suffering or inflicting pain. Above all the differentiation that now sets in imposes a much greater burden on the female, not only in the physical but also in the psychical respect. While the male reproductive function consists of sadistically mastering the sexual object and is completed with the attainment of organ pleasure, it is only the beginning of the complicated activity that devolves upon the female for the purpose of maintaining the species. From that moment on the role of woman as a sexual being is transformed in the sense that, over and above her individual trends and aspirations, she becomes the 'transitory bearer of the germ plasma' (Freud). The psychical task of the woman in relation to these new obligations consists in overcoming the conflict that now arises between the 'ego libidinal' and reproductive trends. We have already seen in our discussion of the psychology of the phallic phase that the discovery of the lack of the penis is accompanied by an 'ego libidinal' narcissistic wound, and we have noted how the compensatory trends are expressed in the young girl's childish wishful fantasies.

The conflict between the ego and the object cathexes also takes place in normal psychical life, and the way it is dealt with provides a yardstick of mental health.

The nature of woman's reproductive function makes these conflicts more complicated than they are in the male and therefore creates a greater disposition to neurotic illnesses.

The overriding picture of the course of this reproductive activity is composed of a number of major, incisive events, all of which have a common characteristic. For both body and soul they are traumas, involving a rupture of continuity and pain.

Both physically and mentally they make new demands on the female, bring about a change in external and internal relations, and impose on her an organic and psychic ordeal. In the physical field these shattering events are of a bloody and traumatic nature, and that applies to menstruation, defloration, impregnation, confinement, and the menopause.

In the life of the human male there is basically only one biologically conditioned situation that involves an increased demand as a result of the establishment of a new sexual objective. That is puberty, the difficulties of which for the male consist exclusively of adaptation of the previous psychical constellations and infantile attitudes to the demands of the new sexual aim. The psychical task consists of completing and superseding lower levels of development.

For the woman things are different. In the first place, puberty is made more difficult because of psychical conflicts, at the heart of which there is the first appearance of menstruation. Also, the periodicity of menstruation means on every occasion a return in more or less attenuated form of its first traumatic incidence and at the same time a repetition in reminiscence of that first situation that was associated with so many difficulties; there is, as it were, a continually repeated puberty with its struggles.

In the second place, every one of the above-mentioned sexual experiences calls, just like puberty, for a psychical regrouping, an adaptation to a new biologically imposed sexual function, a new order in the libidinal economy.

CHAPTER FIVE

The psychology of puberty

According to Helene Deutsch's thinking, adolescence was the point at which 'femaleness' becomes firmly established. It might well be, however, that she was mistaken in thinking that human bisexuality lasts as long as she supposed. Instead, as analysts like Melanie Klein (see, for example, Brierley, 1936) and Karen Horney were afterwards to postulate, early primary vaginal feelings may help account for later feminine features (Barnett, 1966; Lorand, 1939). Although Helene Deutsch had observed that 'from earliest infancy distinctive features appear in boys and girls' (chapter one; see also chapter four) she still maintained that femininity was some kind of retreat from disappointed masculine trends.

In my view, development from the so-called phallic phase, of which Helene Deutsch, following Freud, had made so much, may be relatively secondary.[1] This might sound almost a theological point; but it had the implication that feminine castration anxiety might be relegated to a far lesser role, and therefore one would have to rec-

consider Helene Deutsch's earlier proposition that the
pre-genital phases in both sexes were identical. If her
work unwittingly helped reinforce sexual stereotyping,
as some would argue, it would not be the first time that
an apparent innovation had unanticipated reactionary
implications.

Entirely aside from the issue of penis envy, in discuss-
ing the beginning of menstruation, which is still considered a special problem (Koff, Rierdan, & Jacobson,
1981), she was touching on what some would now think
of as at least one possible fantasy. As recently as Mary
Jane Sherfey's *The Nature and Evolution of Female Sexuality* (1972, pp. 10–11), a writer has vividly recounted
her own initial response to the onset of menses. Later
on, a woman is subject to repeated fluctuations in her
libidinal economy, symbolized by the uncontrollability of
the menstrual flow. It is now well recognized that there
can be psychogenic components in the absence of bleeding (amenorrhea), as well as excessive pain (dysmenor-
rhea); and even organic gynaecologic problems are
known to have secondary psychological consequences
(Sturgis, 1962).

In another contemporary context, such as the use of
birth control pills, we are only just beginning to learn
about the emotional and somatic consequences of interferences with menstrual periods. Other forms of contraception also have psychological implications, to add
to the age-old quandary about the nature of pre-men-
strual stress, which is still not well understood today.
Thinkers of many different schools, however, seem to
agree that women are more prone to depression, and
that loss would appear to have a specific meaning for
them.

Helene Deutsch explicitly acknowledged, if only in
passing, the special role that 'cultural conditions' play
for women, as opposed to men, in enforcing a long delay
between the attainment of sexual maturity and the possibility of satisfaction. This would help to account, she

believed, for the exceptional place of fantasy life in the young girl's experiences. Although as a theorist her orientation was overwhelmingly intra-psychic, she realized that a feminine code of abstinence could have consequences for the attraction of the forbidden.

Among the pubertal fantasies that still sound plausible, Helene Deutsch mentions the 'parthenogenetic' one of a self-produced child. Later she would use the idea of immaculate conception to help account for mothering (Deutsch, 1965, pp. 193–194), as well as illegitimate pregnancies (Deutsch, 1944, p. 323). In general, she thought of intellectual production 'in the male manner' as a sublimation of this aspiration for independence. She considered herself as having been spiritually fertilized by her contact with Freud, but it would have been better had she been able to see how social forces could play a role in 'the sporadic appearance of individual women whose intellectual achievements are completely original'.

Whether puberty represents, as Helene Deutsch thought, a new consolidation of instinctual drives or, instead, a reaffirmation of earlier feminine tendencies that she may have underestimated hinges on a basic decision about the primary significance of feminine erotic wishes. If the young woman understands in some way the nature of her future unique abilities, it becomes superfluous to hypothesize the necessity of the mature woman's transferring earlier pre-genital trends to the vagina.

Psychoanalytic experience has taught us that the differentiation between the sexes is definitely completed only at puberty. Previously the immature individual, in spite of the preparation that has taken place during the infantile phases, has lived under the aegis of bisexuality; sexual wishes and fantasies have not been completely directed to heterosexual object-choice. Puberty and its struggles show that the final phase of infantile development, with its 'push towards passivity' in the sense of femininity, is not completely effective. Among other things, actual disappointments, particularly those connected with the wish for a child, may be responsible for this. It seems as if a reactivation of the abandoned wish for the penis had already begun in the pre-pubertal phase. For the task of puberty once again consists in overcoming the male-oriented component of sexual life. These male tendencies now link up with the clitoral masturbation of the pre-pubertal stage. We already know that this organ represents the penis not only biogenetically but also psychologically in the girl's fantasies.

At puberty clitoral masturbation is normally given up, and the renunciation of this erogenous zone is identical with the giving up in favour of complete femininity of the male trends associated with that organ. This pubertal renunciation does not take place without struggles, at the heart of which there is the major event of the first menstruation.

Analytic experience has shown us that to the girl's unconscious the first appearance of blood is—in one determining aspect—a punishment for clitoral masturbation. At an earlier stage, as we have seen, the idea in the young girl's unconscious that she had had a penis, which was taken away from her—that she had been castrated, in fact—played an important role. This fantasized 'castration' was connected with the guilt of masturbation. With the giving up of the clitoris as an organ of excitation and with the appearance of menstruation one might say that a real castration had taken place, in the sense of the loss of a pleasurable organ that had functioned as a surrogate penis.

Thus the first menstruation involves a 'narcissistic wound' in the sense of the final loss of a desired and painfully missed part of the body. That the reactive trends to retain the penis (clitoris) that then arise are plainly expressed is a definite fact: in many cases the clitoral masturbation that had been given up returns only at the time of menstruation, to an extent as a reminiscence of the first appearance of blood and the renunciation of the clitoris as a pleasure-providing organ associated with it. The narcissistic wound of the loss of the penis at puberty is wiped out by a compensatory satisfaction of the ego.

The activity of the ductless glands that now sets in and the development of secondary sexual characteristics lead to the development of new feminine physical charms, and the narcissistic libido shifts from the genitals to the whole body (Harnik, 1923)[2]. In this way the narcissistic trends have put themselves secondarily in the service of the function of reproduction.

To the girl's conscious the beginning of menstruation means attainment of her long-desired sexual maturity and the prospect, the possibility, of bearing the child that will compensate her completely for all her narcissistic wounds. But in contrast to this the actual fact of menstruation leaves the promise unfulfilled and is a bitter disappointment. Biologically menstruation means a fertilization that has not taken place; it was hardly known among primitive women who were prematurely mated and impregnated immediately after the first ovulation.

Thus psychologically menstruation means to the unconscious what it in fact is biologically and is later consciously regarded as a failure to have a child. So it becomes the second great disappointment, and this time from the point of view of specifically female trends.

Psychoanalytic experience has shown us that a child compensates woman for the lack of a penis and that the narcissistic satisfaction of the child wipes out the narcissistic wound.

Typical menstrual complaints[3]

We have now learned that menstruation involves two wounds—no child and no penis—and so it comes as no surprise to us that it is especially apt to produce reactions of disappointment. In our cultural conditions hardly any women can be expected to react to menstruation without symptoms of some sort.

Analysis of these symptoms, which range from the mildest complaints to severe mental and physical illness, shows them to be based on two narcissistic injuries, 'no penis and no child', which draw their contents now from one, now from the other. The constant concomitant phenomena of menstruation—still within the borders of the physiological—include headaches, depression, irritability, as well as more or less severe dysmenorrhoea.

Analysis has regularly shown that of these typical symptoms the headache is associated with the castration complex, in the sense that the head is the seat of the intellect and is the embodiment of male proficiency. Each of these symptoms has, of course, several determinants, and its meaning varies from individual to individual. A fuller account of analytic experiences would take us too far afield.

The psychical symptoms very characteristically bear the mark of reactions to the loss that has been suffered and can range all the way to the clinical picture of severe melancholia. Also, the aggravation of melancholia and the depressive phases in the course of mania during menstruation are known to every psychiatrist. These depressions are all under the aegis of the double loss, 'no child and no penis'.

These psychical reactions can lose their menstrual nature and appear in the intervals. In these cases the connection with menstruation can be established only psychoanalytically.

We have already mentioned that puberty revives abandoned infantile positions of the libido and that the fantasy life that proliferates at this period still stands under the aegis of regressive factors, i.e., is accompanied by a return to infantile attitudes. So we shall not be surprised to find that the objects of the fantasy structures in the unconscious have the fates of infantile objects, i.e., the parents. Though the libido is now centred on the genitals, it still includes tendencies that enable the mobilization of abandoned pre-genital organizations to be detected.

Thus analysis enables us to discern the link between the symptoms closely associated with these fantasies and infantile residues.

The dysmenorrhoeic complaints mentioned above go hand in hand with unconscious fantasies of confinement, which for their part are under the aegis of the Oedipus complex.

Analysis of the amenorrhoea that occurs so frequently—particularly among young girls—has generally revealed fantasies of pregnancy as their unconscious content (Eisler, 1923).

The way in which genital bleeding is used as an hysterical conversion symptom or is psychically applied to various purposes of defence, flight, or demonstration, etc., falls outside the framework of this study (Groddeck).

The nature of the relationship between the somatic and the physical in these cases is a matter that cannot be discussed here. Also, the nature of these relationships is still too problematical and unexplained.

Difficulties of puberty

As we have seen, this first event of puberty, which is so crucial in the life of the female, lies at the heart of the difficulties that arise with the new tasks that confront her as she enters womanhood with the attainment of sexual maturity.

Her future destiny as a woman, in the sense of her psychical health and possibility of happiness, depends on the outcome of this first great decisive struggle—i.e., on her overcoming her male-directed pre-pubertal tendencies and on the favourable inception of readiness for reproduction—

though, as we shall see, this finally establishes itself only later. The task now is not only to get over the narcissistic wound of lost masculinity but also to dispose satisfactorily of the infantile residues of the pre-genital phases of development and of the earlier object choice, which have now become unserviceable and have inhibiting and disturbing effects on her sexual freedom of movement.

Difficulties also result from cultural conditions, which for the female in particular interpose a long delay of varying duration between the attainment of sexual maturity and the possibility of satisfaction. The requirement to adapt completely to the real renunciation is generally taken more seriously by girls than it is by men. The requirement of complete renunciation forces the young girl back into fantasy life from the normal aspiration for the fulfilment of awakened sexual desires, with the result that subsequent reversion to greater real freedom can be made more difficult. The difficulties that then appear take many forms: abnormal character formations develop, object choice becomes harder, neurotic symptoms—above all frigidity and certain strongly psychically determined forms of sterility—appear, and relations to the child both before and after birth become more difficult, etc. In short, difficulties arise in all situations that call for a fully feminine attitude. Thus the mere fact of the ban on the realization of sexual wishes in the early period of abstinence can result in that ban henceforward being associated with all sexual stirrings, with only the breaking of the ban having any special attractiveness (Freud, 1918a). Any kind of sexual sensibility is henceforward possible only on condition that it is forbidden; hence the choice of love objects against the wishes of the parents or the ability to enjoy the sexual act only outside the social sexual code, etc. There are women, for instance, who under the influence of this conditioning of their love life remain frigid in their marriage and react with strongly positive feelings to any kind of extra-marital, i.e. forbidden, intercourse.

Typical fantasies of puberty

Certain typical fantasies that begin at the time of puberty and fill the period of sexual maturity until the possibility of real satisfaction arises belong to the permanent armoury of women and, when they lead to a more pronounced withdrawal from the outside world and to intense introversion in a fantasy world, become the point of departure of neurotic disturbances and certain character formations. These fantasies, even when they do not lead to pathological reactions, are so characteristic of female nature that they cannot be ignored in the present context.

Some I describe as parthenogenetic fantasies, and others as whore fantasies.

Both are rooted in the Oedipus and castration complexes, and further reactions arise as a result of the 'no child, no penis' wound suffered with the appearance of menstruation, which we discussed above.

The parthenogenetic fantasy[4] is as follows: 'I possess a child out of myself alone, I am its mother and its father. I need and want no man to produce this child.'

In a certain type of woman with strong masculine tendencies this fantasy characteristically becomes a perfectly conscious wish. Sometimes, though rarely, one of these women will fulfil it by the production of a child with the aid of the 'first suitable man she comes across'—his role being reduced to that of fertilization only.

The development of this fantasy is completely analogous to the biological process to which it owes its name. Just as parthenogenesis arose out of an emphigenic, i.e., bisexual, form of reproduction with a regression of the act of fertilization, so was the parthenogenetic fantasy child originally conceived bisexually by the father in the oedipal constellation and was transformed into a parthenogenetic child only as a reaction to the menstruation wound.

This fantasy contains a number of variously oriented wish-fulfilments. It frees the woman from part of the guilt feeling rooted in the Oedipus complex in that it denies that the child originates with the father. It attenuates the castration wound by replacing the penis that has been finally lost with another enlargement of the body ego produced by the woman herself; the self-produced child gives her the narcissistic satisfaction of being able to say: 'What a man can do I can do too.'

In sublimation this fantasy expresses itself in the aspiration for independence and in the creation of 'parthenogenetic children', intellectual production in the male manner. But in most cases there is a demonstration of the impossibility of completely realizing these aspirations; for other psychical trends in woman—to which we shall return later—result in their intellectual children never being able to bear the marks of parthenogenesis and coming about only as a result of an act of male intellectual fertilization.

True, the sporadic appearance of individual women whose intellectual achievements are completely original cannot be denied; but we are trying to obtain an unprejudiced psychological understanding of why this is possible only in exceptional cases.

In our analysis we have gained the impression that the predominance of 'parthenogenetic' fantasies, as well as the reactions to these fantasies in the shaping of destinies (tendencies to intellectual activity) and symptom formation, are characteristic of a certain type of woman. This type has reacted to the narcissistic wound of the loss of the penis in puberty with a kind of displacement 'upwards from below' and has replaced the missing organ with overvaluation of the intellect.

The second group of fantasies, which we have called whore fantasies, is also rooted in the Oedipus and castration complexes; they too arise in connection with the events of puberty and are merely another way in which the disappointment we have described expresses itself. It says: 'I walk the streets, in my abasement I give myself to every man.' It contains the reaction to the disappointed love of the father: 'If father won't have me, I'll give myself to everyone.' In situations in later life in which a woman is really scorned by a man this psychological determining may often become a conscious cause of resorting to prostitution: 'Since he despises me, I'll despise myself.'

Also, a kind of 'over-moral' sexual education intended to protect the young girl from infringing the ban may produce in her the idea that her sexual curiosity and desire are identical with whorishness; hence she associates every erotic desire with the idea of being a whore.

This fantasy also draws its content from the castration complex. It seeks to fulfil the wish for revenge for the castration that has been suffered. This expresses itself in the tendency to take something from all men's bodies in coitus and contemptuously throw it away, in contrast to the maternal tendencies of normal women, who also want to take something from the man in intercourse, but only to keep it in the form of a child and then present it again to the man in this new form.

We have seen that one type of woman seeks consolation and compensation for the genital wound in over-valuation of the intellect and in masculine intellectual aspirations, making the 'head', so to speak, a surrogate organ and creating a parthenogenetic child in fantasy.

In contrast to this, the type that is more inclined to prostitution fantasies and their realization seems to seek satisfaction for wounded narcissism in the libidinal cathexis of the whole body (that is, in the transfer of libido from the genitals to the whole body, as we explained above)—in other words, derives satisfaction from its own physical beauty.

It seems clear to us that both types of fantasy conflict with 'motherhood' and do not lead to a favourable relationship with the male. Their further development thus influences woman's normal relationship with the reproductive function, though it must be emphasized that there are no sharp boundaries in psychical life and that, for instance, the most intense motherliness can co-exist with the most luxuriant prostitution fantasies, and *vice versa*.

There is another typical pubertal fantasy that we must not ignore; that is, the rape fantasy, the content of which is rooted in the idea that the sexual act involves the forcing of the woman by the man. This fantasy again diminishes the guilt feeling attached to the forbidden act, for if something is done by violence the victim is innocent—thus making it possible to fulfil wishes in fantasy without burdening the conscience. In addition to that, the first genital bleeding once again regressively activates the infantile conception of coitus, which in the child's fantasy is almost invariably sadistic in nature and is represented as a cruel and bloody act. On the other hand, the rape fantasy also conceals a presentiment of the bloody act of defloration. Pathological expression of this fantasy often takes the form of the young girl's fear of burglars and false claims by hysterics that they have been raped. This attitude of masochistic expectation is the outcome of the adoption of the passive-feminine stance; all the instinctual manifestations of woman are under the aegis of the latter. We also see that the psychological task of puberty and menstruation also consists in the establishment of a new passivity drive that prepares the woman for masochistically suffering man's sadistic onslaught.

Instincts and their vicissitudes at puberty

Thus the girl's pubertal task is twofold. Male-active, sadistically oriented infantile trends have to give way to a female passive-masochistic position, and a new erogenous zone has to be erected that puts itself at the disposal of these passive trends. Both achievements represent the last act in a process that, as we saw above, was already being prepared in the final phase of infantile sexual development as the conclusion of the infantile genital organization. The task now is the definitive renunciation of the clitoris as an erogenous zone and the transfer to the vagina of the passive-anal trends that by a process of regression already became active in the first, post-phallic phase of passivity.

These two requirements make the process of libido development in women much more difficult than it is in man.

In men the progress of the phallic phase does not take place through a complicated process of repression, but depends on an acceptance of something that exists and on willingness to use the spontaneous urge. The task consists of coping with the oedipal position involved and overcoming the guilt feeling connected with it.

Over and above this, the girl has a double task:

1. She must renounce the masculinity bound up with the clitoris and transform the sadistic trends associated with this into masochistic trends (the passivity drive).
2. In changing from the phallic to the vaginal phase, she must discover the new genital organ.

Both tasks are finally completed only in the sex act and, what is more, in being masochistically mastered by the penis in the act of defloration and in the discovery of a new source of pleasure in the vagina under the active guidance of the male organ.

But before the last act is completed, the female libido must attain a position of readiness on the maturation of which the success of the sex act from the point of view of the female vaginal phase ultimately depends.

As we have seen, the preparations for womanliness began in the early infantile stages of development and manifested themselves in the normal oedipal attitude by way of identification with the mother. But, in spite of their bisexual constitution, the psychical disposition of the small girl in all phases of infantile development differs from that of the small boy and indicates that the discovery of the vagina is only the last act in a gradually developing process. Observation of children's games makes the passive-feminine attitude of the young girl unmistakably evident.

The dreams of the latency period as well as the fantasies of the pre-pubertal stage reveal the masochistic trend of the rape wishes contained in them long before their intensive cathexis at puberty. That it is not just educational and identificational processes that are involved here is shown by observation of the animal kingdom, in which males attempt to cover and females crouch long before reproductive activity has begun. We mention this to emphasize the fact that the highly complicated psychological differentiation between man and woman is constitutionally prefigured and that the final 'passivity boost' in the woman is also affected by the inhibitory influences of sex hormones.

Our knowledge of the psychological mechanism of the 'passivity boost' is summed up in the definition we quoted above, which was supplied by Freud. But how the suppression of the male-active tendency in women comes about, from where the drive is initiated and how the suppression of masculinity becomes identical with the attainment of the feminine position are matters about which we are not yet clear.

We know that intensification of the sexual drive is connected with increased activity in general. Thus animal-breeders, for instance, report an unusual increase in motility both of male and female animals when the sexual drive increases, which can lead to violence and killing.

This increase in aggressive tendencies with the appearance of sexual maturity is simply explained by the intensification of the drive, the quantitative increase of which is equivalent to an increase in activity, for the drive is 'always active' and the more intensively it appears, the more actively will it be reflected in behaviour.

The increased intensity of the drive at puberty finds both girl and boy at the same active-male phallic phase of development, which in both cases makes its appearance bound to the penis or surrogate penis, the clitoris.

In the male the intensification of the drive goes hand in hand with the trend to conquer the object in the outside world. The activity of the phallic phase can be said to be reinforced—the new or reinforced function presses for the creation of a new organ to be at its disposal. In the male this organ is already present, the new task confronting him is demonstrated by its tendency to growth and above all by the tendency that manifests itself in him to find and possess himself of an object in the outside world. At this phase the penis becomes a capturing organ and its task is sadistic—in the sense of an active-libidinal taking possession of the object. Only when the relationship to the sex object exceeds the limits of taking possession of it in the sex act, i.e., when the aim is hostile destruction, is it 'sadistic' in the sense of the pre-genital phases. In the genital phase sadistic and active and male are identical.

The same active tendency of the intensified sex drive in puberty, which in man manifests itself in his masculinity, also applies to woman. The drive is always active, and its active tendencies increase with the increase in its intensity. Analytic study of the course of development of the female libido shows us unmistakably that in the female, just as in the male, the development of puberty is accompanied by an increase in activity, i.e., an 'activity boost', and that thus our familiar 'passivity boost' represents only a last act in a complicated process.

In the female, as in the male, the active tendency has a 'rectilinear' (Freud) effect in reinforcing the phallic phase. The clitoris, like the penis, thrusts 'in masculine fashion' into the outside world. But the organ that was sufficient for autoerotic activity now fails as an organ of conquest in relation to the outside world. The actively oriented function fails for lack of an executive organ that the woman is unable to provide, and the lack of the penis that now manifests itself—one might say definitively—confronts the woman's phallic-active masculine trends with a wall of frustration from which her active trends bounce back. The next phase in the destiny of this trend is known to us from elsewhere. It turns against itself, i.e., changes into its partner, masochism, and activity is transformed into passivity.

In his paper on 'The economic problem of masochism', Freud (1924c) sees in female masochism a typical instance of primary, erogenous masochism, i.e., of the primary destructive drive at work in the organism, which remains libidinally bound in the object while the chief component of the death drive is discharged outwards in the form of sadism.

The mechanism of the 'passivity boost' we assumed above, which because of the lack of an appropriate organ could not discharge the urge to conquest into the outside world but remained in the organism and took the individual herself as its object, would thus be a complementary application of Freud's assumption. The fact, however, is that its mobilization or manifestation in the passivity boost of puberty comes about only when the sadistically outward turned drive turns inward in secondary repression as a consequence of the impossibility of discharging it. In this sense the female 'passivity boost' is a typical example of what Freud calls secondary masochism, which arises only out of regressive sadism. It is added to the primary erogenous sadism, and the two together result in the 'masochistic position' of woman.

With the 'passivity boost' the previously active 'organ', the clitoris, is destined for destruction. It has to retreat, because it cannot keep pace with the increased demands for activity. In the new masochistic phase it succumbs to self-castration, and from this point on the masochistic position is maintained in fantasies of defloration and rape.

In the psychology of female puberty the phenomenon I have described as the activity boost regularly manifests itself physiologically. All girls go through a phase in which their bisexuality receives a masculine reinforcement. This appears above all in a reinforced capacity for sublimation, in the manifestations of homosexuality that now take place, and in their whole mental and physical deportment. Observation of this strikingly regular intensification of masculinity just before the development of femininity became the point of departure of my theoretical ideas.

This activity boost, then, goes hand-in-hand with the mobilization of the 'masculinity complex' that arose in the phallic phase and is now destined for final extinction. What happens to it in practice depends on the way with which it is dealt, and if this is unfavourable, the result can be 'masculine' character formations on the one hand or the pubertal neuroses associated with the castration complex on the other.

The mechanism described above corresponds to the path by which the female attitude of readiness is attained. The establishment of the new, passive erogenous zone takes place in the discovery of the vagina as an organ of pleasure in the act of being masochistically mastered by the penis, which becomes the signpost to this new source of pleasure.

NOTES

1. In 1932 Deutsch pointed out that in her 1925 book she had spoken of 'a "swing towards passivity" in girls, at the centre of which lies the desire of an anal child by the father. Already at that time I pointed out that this swing towards passivity is really a regressive process, the regression being to a phase *before* the phallic organization, which is identical in boys and girls. In my view we have been too much absorbed by the processes in the phallic phase. . . .'

2. Harnik also came to the conclusion on the basis of his experiences that to the unconscious the first menstrual bleeding means castration.

3. We shall not here discuss the numerous neurotic symptoms that appear in the form of menstrual disturbances. The reader is referred to the valuable paper by J. M. Eisler (1923).

4. An interesting example of this fantasy has been handed down to us by the nun Antoinette Bourignon, who lived in the seventeenth century. She developed religious-scientific theories according to which humanity would attain salvation when women attained the capacity to produce children completely on their own without male assistance. 'Cet état d'innocence n'est pas celui de l'asexualité, mais une sorte d'hermaphroditisme' [This state of innocence is not that of asexuality but a kind of hermaphrod-

itism]. According to her biographers, her intellectual productivity was accompanied by physical pains, which were just like those of labour. *'Elle ressentit de grandes douleurs corporelles et comme de pressantes tranchées d'un enfantement'* [She felt great physical pains and feelings akin to the contractions of labour] (see Reinach, *Cultes, Mythes et Religions: une Mystique au XVIIième Siècle*).

CHAPTER SIX

The act of defloration

The title of this chapter in itself highlights how different the world Helene Deutsch grew up in was from our own. In late-nineteenth-century Poland ritual defloration, especially among the peasantry, was still a common practice; and in that whole era virginity had a meaning that may be difficult to appreciate today. For certain social classes, for example, a woman would be considered unmarriageable unless she were still a virgin. Shyness and reserve in a woman, and the need to be courted, could be especially attractive, making a man feel he was a conqueror in overcoming obstacles. What is now widely regarded as a sexual double-standard was once firmly embedded in a whole psychosocial framework.

Venereal disease was medically more difficult to treat, and syphilitic insanity was still one of mankind's great scourges. (Our own experience with AIDS should be a reminder of what earlier times had to adjust to.) During World War I Helene Deutsch's early psychiatric mentor, Professor Julius Wagner von Jauregg (a contemporary of Freud's), developed malarial treatment for general paresis; in 1927 he became the first and only psychiatrist ever to win a Nobel Prize. Entirely aside from the specific horror of venereal infection, contraception was harder then and pregnancy (or abortions) more dangerous. The real counterpart to male castration fear may be the feminine anxiety of injury to her own genitalia (Jacobson, 1976, p. 537; Deutsch, 1945, p. 111). The so-called sexual freedom in our own time has to be put into its cultural context.

At the time Helene Deutsch was writing, modern anthropology had just begun to flourish. It was then commonplace to compare the practices of living non-literate peoples with the customs of early ancestors of man. Complex societies were thought to have 'evolved' from simpler cultures. Freud himself repeatedly spoke of non-literates as primitive and savage, phrases bound to offend those who sought to emancipate anthropology from nineteenth-century ethnocentrism. Yet for us to consider ourselves more cosmopolitan than the society from which Helene Deutsch came would be to repeat the error of mistakenly believing in the superiority of a later culture to an earlier one.

T he supreme manifestation of readiness for being masochistically possessed is the male sadistic intervention, the act of defloration, which is the second bloody event in the sexual life of woman.

The pleasure–pain that has to be undergone is embodied in the hymen, which represents in material form the whole of the passive-masochistic ordeal.

In spite of various attempts at explanation, we do not fully understand its phylogenetic significance. The fact is that in the function it exercises it is peculiar to the human species. Attempts have been made to relate to it the fold of skin found in higher animals, but this is connected only with the position of the animals concerned in coitus, it is permanent, and it serves the purposes of preventing the penis from slipping out.

One cannot avoid suspecting that the hymen in its existing form and function is a product of breeding, which originated in the male drive to sadistic conquest and in the female desire for masochistic suffering. The circumstance that numerous customs and practices of savage tribes aim at increasing the pleasure of the sex act by inflicting greater pain on the one hand and suffering it on the other would seem to be evidence in favour of this possibility. One of these practices is infibulation, which consists of restoring the no longer existent hymen by sewing up—a custom that is perhaps the best pointer to the hymen's origin.

In our discussion of the girl's psychical reaction to the first menstruation we saw that her psychical task lay in working through the traumatic experience of disappointment.

To the woman defloration, just like the first menstruation, means not only an unmitigated disappointment, since the expected sexual pleasure is not felt, but is also a narcissistic wound.

Only after the psychical mechanism has succeeded in overcoming this disappointment and creating compensations does the woman become a fully enjoying partner, a completely mature sexual being. In the physical respect this state of maturity is reflected in the transfer to the vagina of the excitability hitherto centred on the clitoris. This process, which takes place only gradually by way of a highly complicated mechanism, is exposed to various difficulties, and its failure leads to many neurotic disturbances. In his paper 'The taboo of virginity' Freud (1918a), basing himself on certain rites practised by primitive tribes, throws light on the psychology of the act of defloration.

The rules and ceremonies involved testify to the fact that among primitive tribes defloration is not only just as grave an event as it is among civilized peoples, but that it is also the object of religious commandments and prohibitions, i.e., is subject to taboo. The rules divide the first sexual intercourse in marriage into two parts, of which the first is a ritual defloration carried out manually or instrumentally, but at all events not by the husband, while the subsequent sex act is left to him.

The psychological significance of the taboo has been shown (Freud, 1912–13) to be that it averts a danger that the primitive fears. The practices associated with the act of defloration indicate that by them the primitive seeks to avoid a threatening danger, and that the purpose underlying the rules and regulations is to avert the threat overhanging the bridegroom. In contrast to these primitive customs, the demands of our own culture require a girl to maintain her virginity until marriage and regard defloration as the exclusive right and privilege of the husband. In spite of this divergence of moral requirements, psychological discoveries about civilized women have enlightened us about the real dangers—real in the sense of psychical reality—from which the primitive seeks to protect himself.

It is generally recognized that for a woman the first sex act, corresponding with defloration, is a disappointment, which, assuming favourable psychical conditions, is only gradually overcome. If it is not overcome, the woman remains frigid, as she almost invariably is in the act of defloration.

This initial frigidity generally comes under analytical observation only in those cases in which it has become permanently stabilized as a neurotic symptom. Explaining it by the pain that was inflicted as well as the difficulty of access to the virginal genitals, etc., turns out to be insufficient, as is shown also by the fact that the frigidity can continue even when these factors no longer apply. Analytic experience has taught us that the act of defloration mobilizes the same never completely overcome traces of infantile feelings that were mobilized by menstruation and that the bloody destruction of an organ revives the psychical wound of the castration complex. Thus to the woman the act of defloration becomes another narcissistic wound, and hostile revenge feelings directed at the man prevent loving tenderness from being complete. If these awakened hostile feelings are not overcome by a favourable attitude to loving, it will manifest itself as frigidity in the sex act. Hence the psychological explanation of 'woman's subjection' to the first man can be on two different lines.

In the first place, it can arise through the positive component of the struggle between two opposing trends; to suppress the hostility, the love relationship must have been at an intense level. Similarly, a great psychical effort must have been required to overcome the young girl's sexual resistance. These are generally the two decisive factors in woman's 'subjection'.

But it can also be the hostile trend, the unfulfilled desire for vengeance, that causes the woman to cling to the man who first mobilized her hostility in the act of defloration.

This enables us to understand the psychological reasons for the protective rituals of primitives.

We have now seen how many psychological difficulties have to be overcome on the way to attaining full sexual maturity. If the pubertal and post-pubertal period are made difficult by the necessity of overcoming infantile residues and their traces in fantasies, the further path is complicated by the intervention of the sexual partner. The struggle between tender and hostile feelings now takes place in relation to him. Also, the last traces of past stages of development try to break through again before they give way to the attainment of complete maturity in the sense of the primacy of the vagina as the leading sexual organ.

We have seen that the act of defloration reactivates the stage of development that manifests itself in the castration complex. The narcissistic wound suffered by the woman in that respect is mobilized by it and results in frigidity, i.e., withdrawal of love from the partner. Experience shows us that even if the course of development has been favourable, leading to a 'passivity boost', the reaction to the act of defloration remains under the aegis of protest, and the completely female attitude is consolidated only later with the establishment of the new erogenous zone.

For the woman's conscious the disappointment of defloration lies in the pain experienced and in the failure of the accustomed clitoral satisfaction, the dethronement of the pleasure function of the clitoris, and the bloody destruction of an organ situated in the genitals, which now acquires the meaning of the penis that has again been destroyed, as the clitoris was on the appearance of the first menstrual blood.

Only with the genitalization of the vagina—that is, with the creation of a new organ cathected with sufficient quantities of libido—is the woman consoled for the losses she has suffered.

CHAPTER SEVEN

Psychology of the sex act

Early psychoanalysis held that the libidinal phases leading to the ideal of maturity constitute a sequence that
oscillates back and forth. Distant satisfactions leave
their residue, and regressive tendencies co-exist with
higher levels of development. For the woman as for the
man, the attaining of the post-ambivalent phase of normality was thought of as a difficult attainment.

Helene Deutsch might have been wrong in her view
that only 'vague presentiments' of the vagina as an
organ of pleasure are known to the small girl and still
have been right in a sense about the importance of penis
envy. For even if envy of the male is now seen by some
not to have been a biological factor but to have had
sociological origins, logically it is possible for a woman
to be fully satisfied with her feminine capacities and at
the same time still be jealous of male prerogatives.

Conceptually this chapter is a *tour de force*. Entirely
in terms of libido theory she accounts for the specific
nature of the female orgasm. It is, in Ferenczi's phrase,

'amphimictic'—a telescoping and merging of all the pre-genital drives of earlier phases. Helene Deutsch makes the original suggestion that a woman can partly achieve sexual gratification through identification with a man's penis. In her account of the complete harmony of coitus, one is reminded of Plato's myth about part of humanity, split from its original unity into two distinct sexes, ever-lastingly striving for the ecstasy of reunion.

For the woman, unlike the man, the sex act can have a sequel in pregnancy and labour. It is sometimes mis-takenly thought that it is a recent idea that processes of giving birth are an aspect of female sexuality (see, for example, Erikson, 1980; Kitzinger, 1978). Maternity was, according to Helene Deutsch, so crucial to femin-inity that she proposed a psychological explanation for the different reactions of men and women to post-coital relaxation. (She later extended the significance of a woman's simultaneously playing the role of mother and child to female homosexuality as well—Deutsch, 1965, pp. 165–89).

Helene Deutsch contrasted men and women sexually: 'the man actively conquers a piece of the world and by this route achieves the happiness of the primal con-dition', whereas 'the woman in the passively experienced act of incorporation introjects a piece of the objective world which she draws into herself'. But she also thought that this characteristic difference helped to account for the strengths and capacities appropriate for each sex. She would later propose that one of a woman's greatest sources of talent—and here she was speaking with pride of her profession as a psychoanalyst—lies in the ability to identify with others (see, for example, Deutsch, 1944, pp. 130ff). Of course Helene Deutsch was living at a time when, at least in the case of the middle class, women had to live primarily through others; yet motherliness and vicarious living are also intrinsically interconnected.

The psychological mechanism of the shift of the sensitive zone from the clitoris to the vagina is a complicated one, and the fact that many women never give up clitoral excitation in favour of the vagina bears witness to the difficulty of the transition. This is first achieved in the sex act, and psychological understanding of the significance of the act from the point of view of the female libido is necessary if the process is to be intelligible.

The male part in the sex act consists essentially of the discovery of the vagina in the outside world and its sadistic conquest. The way to this is shown him by the pressure to perform this act of conquest exercised by his genitals, which are already well known to him.

The female individual, however, has to discover this new sexual organ in her own body, and, as we have already mentioned, the discovery takes place in the act of being masochistically mastered by the penis.

The final task of the completely achieved female attitude is not the satisfaction in the sex act of the infantile wish for a penis, but the successful discovery of the vagina as an organ of pleasure, the exchange of the wish for a penis for the real and equivalent possession of the vagina. To the woman, as Ferenczi (1938) has stated in relation to the value of the penis to the male, this newly discovered organ must be a 'miniature of the whole ego', a 'duplication of the ego'.

We try to explain below how this revaluation of the genitals takes place and shows its close connection with the female reproductive function.

We know the sequence according to which the various levels of organization of the libido follow one another, each succeeding element carrying its predecessor along with it, with the result that no level is totally superseded but merely loses its central role. By way of these developmental links the libido at higher levels then tends regressively to arrive at the original positions, which it succeeds in doing by various routes.

The result of this oscillation of the libido between various forms of development is not only that higher phases contain elements of the lower, but also the converse: in its regressions the libido takes with it components of higher phases and interweaves them with the earlier ones—a process that we later detect in fantasy structures and symptoms.

Thus the first oral stage is an auto-erotic one; the object exists neither narcissistically in the ego nor in the outside world. Yet we know from the traces left in the unconscious that weaning means the first narcissistic wound. This results from the fact that the maternal breast—conceived of as part of the infant's own body—is cathected with large quantities of narcissistic libido, as the penis is later. Similarly, discovery of the mother—the first identification of an object—results from the oral satisfaction of the act of sucking.

A first explanation of the riddle of the heterosexual component in the small girl's libido is provided by the earliest stages of development. The love that goes to the father as the object closest to the mother ('the protective male') is supplemented by a large share of the fully sexual libido, which has cathected the maternal breast from the oral zone. Analyses show us that to the unconscious at one stage of development the paternal penis as a sucking organ is equated with the maternal breast. This equation coincides with the idea peculiar to this phase that coitus is a relationship between the mother's mouth and the father's penis and is continued in the theory that birth is a consequence of oral fertilization. In this the mucous membrane of the oral zone is the passive target and the mammary gland the active leading pleasure-producing organ.

In the sadistic–anal phase the penis—in fantasy life—loses its meaning as a sucking organ and becomes an organ of conquest. Coitus is regarded as a sadistic act; in beating fantasies, as we know, the girl either takes over the

father's role or experiences the act masochistically in identification with the mother.

In this phase the anus represents the passive objective
and faeces the leading organ of pleasure, which, like the
mammary gland in the first phase, belongs simultaneously
to the outside world and to the individual's own body.
Ultimately by a shift of cathexis faeces are given the same
narcissistic valuation as the mammary gland in the oral
phase. At this phase the birth fantasy is of the 'anal' child.

The biological analogy between anus and mouth is
known to us. That between breast and penis as active leading organs follows from their function.

It should be an easy task for the further development of
the female libido to seize on the third opening of the female
body, the vagina. For that is a path biologically prefigured
in embryonic development by the fact of common origin in
the cloaca. The penis as organ of stimulation and active
leader for this new erogenous zone could perhaps derive its
function from the equation mammary gland = faeces =
penis.

The difficulty arises from the circumstances that bisexually constituted development interposes the male clitoris
between the anus and the vagina. In the 'phallic' phase of
development the clitoris attracts a large amount of libido
to itself, which it surrenders to the 'female-oriented' vagina
only after arduous and not always successful struggles.
Aggressive activation of passive anal trends initiated
in the phallic phase prepares the way for the later transition to the passively oriented vagina. The task of the last
stage—the transition from the phallic to the vaginal—
which coincides with Abraham's (1945) so-called 'post-
ambivalent' phase—is the most difficult in the course of
development of the female libido.

In the case of the boy the penis is autoerotically discovered in the early infantile period. Also, because of its
exposed position, the boy is able to experience various
actions connected with bodily hygiene, etc., as stimulating.

So the penis can develop into an erogenous zone before the development of its sexual function. All three masturbatory phases are under the aegis of this organ.

During the whole period of development the clitoris—that in fact so inadequate substitute for it—assumes the same significance as the penis. The hidden vagina plays no part, its existence as an organ of pleasure is unknown to the small girl, though perhaps vague presentiments occur. All attempts to explain away a young girl's penis envy by assuring her that she has something of her own end in complete failure, and with good reason, because it is impossible to be satisfied with the possession of something that is not seen or felt.

However, the clitoris as a centre lacks the intensity of the penis—even in the most intensive masturbatory activity it fails to attract to itself as large quantitites of libido as does the penis. More libido therefore remains attached to the original erogenous zones—a circumstance that results in women, even before the beginning of development, remaining more 'polymorphous perverse', more infantile, in character, with 'the whole body a sexual organ' (Freud). In the new boost of development that takes place at puberty this erogeneity of the whole body is reinforced, for the wave of repression that affects the clitoris results in a part of the clitoral libido cathecting the whole body (by way of internal secretion). This, as Ferenczi points out, appears to be important to subsequent development in that it puts women regressively into a position in which in the sexual respect they cling to life in the maternal body.

The task now consists of transferring to the vagina libido from three sources: from (1) the whole body; (2) the most cathected infantile erogenous zones, the oral and the anal; (3) the clitoris, to which a large amount of libido is still attached.

The difficulty lies in the fact that the clitoris does not so easily surrender its goal, that the struggles of puberty are connected with the traumatic event of menstruation, and that this not only revives the castration wound but at the same time represents, in the biological and psychological sense, the disappointing experience of an abortive pregnancy. Each periodic return of menstruation is a reminder, as it were, of the pubertal struggle and a modified repetition of it.

The whole process of menstruation is certainly well adapted to having an eroticizing and preparing affect on the vagina. The task of transferring to it libido from the above-mentioned sources devolves upon the activity of the penis, and that in a twofold manner.

In the first place, the transfer of libido from the whole body takes place in a way that is completely analogous to that of the mammary gland, which actively takes possession of the infant's mouth and concentrates its body libido on that organ. Thus in a transfer 'from above to below' the vagina, under the guiding stimulus of the penis, now takes over the passive role of the sucking mouth in the equation penis = nipple. This oral, sucking activity of the vagina is pre-figured in the whole anatomical structure.

The second task consists in transferring the remaining clitoral libido to the vagina. This libidinal component remains 'male-oriented' even in its vaginal application, i.e., the clitoris renounces its male function in favour of the penis, which is introduced into the body from outside and in wish fulfilment is rated as an organ of the woman's own body.

Just as the clitoris once exercised its 'masculinity' in identification with the paternal penis, so does the vagina take over the role of the clitoris in that it exercises its function partly under the aegis of identification with the partner's penis.

The orgastic activity of the vagina is partly analogous to that of the penis, that is, in its secretional and contractorial element. As in the male, the latter is an 'amphimictic' process of urinal and anal tendencies (Ferenczi), though certainly in a much moderated form. These two partial drives become fully active (as we shall see below) only in the sequel to the sex act, i.e., in pregnancy and labour.

For this element of the vaginal function, which originates by way of identification with the penis and for which the penis represents a possession of the woman's own body, the psychical significance of the sex act lies in the repetition and overcoming of the castration trauma.

The really passive, feminine attitude of the vagina lies in the oral, sucking activity we discussed above.

From this aspect what coitus means to the woman is a re-creation of that first human relationship with the outside world in which the object is incorporated, introjected by the oral route; in other words, a condition of complete unity and harmony in which the boundary between subject and object is wiped out. In this way attainment of the highest genital post-ambivalent phase means a repetition of the first, pre-ambivalent phase.

In relation to the partner the incorporation situation is a repetition of sucking at the mother's breast—in other words, a repetition and overcoming of the trauma of weaning. In the equation penis = mammary gland and in the sucking activity of the vagina coitus fulfils the fantasy of sucking the paternal penis.

The identification between the two partners established in the act of preparation (Ferenczi) now acquires a multiple meaning: above all, that of an identification with the mother (1) through the identification of penis with nipple, and (2) the masochistic experience of this sex act, i.e., repetition of the identification with the mother from the phase in which coitus was regarded as a sadistic act.

Thus in this identification the woman simultaneously plays the role of mother and child—a state of affairs that has a sequel in pregnancy, in which she is simultaneously mother and child.

Thus the partner as an object of maternal libido in the act of sucking becomes the child, assuming that he simultaneously enjoys a transference of the paternal libido (in the sense that the penis means a sucking organ and the partner carries out a sadistic act of conquest). Thus we see that to the woman's unconscious coitus in the last resort means oral incorporation of the father, who is turned into a child and retains this role in the real or fantasized pregnancy that follows.

For the woman Ferenczi's maternal regression in coitus is achieved in the sucking situation. The final act of this regression—the return to the mother's body—which in the case of the man is realized in the act of introjection in coitus, is achieved for the woman in pregnancy in the total identification between mother and child. The whole psychological difference between man and woman in their relationship to the world of objects is expressed in this view of coitus. The man actively conquers a piece of the world and by this route achieves the happiness of the primal condition. That is also the form of his sublimatory trends.

The woman in the passively experienced act of incorporation introjects a piece of the objective world which she draws into herself.

In its role as a sucking and incorporating organ the vagina becomes the container, not of the penis, but of the child. The forces that enable it to carry out this function are drawn, not from the clitoris, but, as we said above, from the libidinal cathexis of the whole body, which is transferred to it by the route now known to us. It becomes a child itself and is thereby cathected with the quantity of narcissistic libido that in the sequel to the act devolves upon the child. It becomes a 'second ego', a miniature of the ego, just as the penis is to the man. If the woman succeeds in establishing this maternal function of the vagina by renouncing the claim of the clitoris to be a penis surrogate, she has completed the development to womanhood. She has attained the post-ambivalent, genital-passive phase.

This maternal attitude to the man in coitus assumes a completely successful sexual development. If she remains fixated at any stage of this development, if her full libido is not available for the establishment of the mother–child relationship, she remains frigid. It is above all the hostile impulses that we met partly in the castration complex and in its reactivation in the act of defloration that prevent complete and definitive surrender to this role.

Just as the acts of preparation serve to establish unity between two egos, so does the embrace in the act of copulation express that complete unity. The orgastic contraction of the vagina is the final expression of that embrace.

Hostile refusal of herself on the woman's part may appear at the preparation stage and can inhibit fore-pleasure, or it may appear in the final stage, the vaginal embrace, in the rejecting genital attitude that says, 'I do not want to make you my child'.

This hostility can express itself in the crude form of vaginismus, through which the man is refused entry, or in the form of penis envy, it can appear in the guise of vaginal cramp in which the penis is held tight and prevented from withdrawing, so that it may be retained.

Only with the establishment of the normal vaginal sexual function does woman become a complete sexual being. In our view, which we shall seek to justify with further arguments below, the female psychical constitution that we have described, woman's ultimate attitude to the object and the psychological meaning of coitus, lead to the conclusion that her sexual and reproductive functions coincide, not in the biological but in the psychological sense.

The difference between the sexes achieves its highest expression in the sex act—in male-active ejection and female-passive retention. We see this in the male ejaculatory function and the female reception of the sperm.

Everything in woman that opposes the passive reception and retention situation is masculine and unfeminine.

Even cruder consideration of the process of coitus plainly illustrates this. While the male act is concluded with the ejection of the genital secretion, even after the flattening out of the coital curve (which takes place more slowly than in the male), there is a distinct tendency on the female part to linger in the incorporation situation.

The overriding characteristic of woman's orgastic ecstasy is this quality of absorption into herself, the urge to remain one with the partner in the sense of incorporating him. Woman's wish to retain the penis in her body in coitus includes not only penis envy but also the tendency to continue one-ness with the child–man. Woman's tender nestling after coitus corresponds psychologically to a state of pregnancy in which the woman—equating man with child—unconsciously believes herself to be and in which she wishes to remain, while the man after the relief of tension tends rather to feel the need for sleep and to be alone.

CHAPTER EIGHT

Frigidity and sterility

Helene Deutsch maintained that the female equivalent of the masculine disturbance of impotence, namely frigidity, was far more frequent, though Freud had not paid a great deal of attention to it. And it would seem, at least from the Index to the *Standard Edition* of Freud's collected writings, that he never entertained the possibility of psychogenic sterility. Yet his general psychological principles have been followed up; it is now often accepted, for example, that there is more than a chance correlation between adoption and ensuing pregnancy.

By itself this chapter suggests that there was something of a psychoanalytic vacuum on the subject of femininity around 1925. Helene Deutsch had all along in *Psychoanalysis of the Sexual Functions of Women* thought of the woman as potentially 'a fully enjoying partner' (see chapter five), whatever the views of the time about female sexual coldness might have been. By 1930 she had come to believe that sexual disturbance is 'emphatically not in direct ratio to the severity of the

neurosis'; according to her, in severe neuroses there can
be no frigidity, and some 'healthy' women are able to
tolerate sexual inhibition well (Deutsch, 1948b, pp. 204,
206; see also 1944, p. 233). (No doubt she was reacting to
some of Wilhelm Reich's simplifications.)

Over the years some of her views changed in important ways. In 1945, for example, six years after Freud's
death, she held that with a clitoris and a vagina the
woman possesses 'two sexual organs' (Deutsch, 1945,
p. 78). She was still addressing herself to the perplex-
ing question of frigidity in a professional panel held as
late as 1960. But by then she had evolved even further,
consistent with the thinking of some other analysts
(Marmor, 1954); now she thought that

the clitoris is the sexual organ, the vagina primarily the
organ of reproduction. . . . The eroticization of the
vagina is a job performed by way of the clitoris and by
the active intervention of man's sexual organ. This
central role of the clitoris is not merely the result of
masturbation, but is a biological destiny. [Deutsch,
1965, p. 360]

In 1925, however, frigidity, like any other neurotic
symptom, was to Helene Deutsch an expression of unconscious conflicts. Not all sex therapists would agree with
this view today; they tend to discount the role of unconscious forces in favour of other significant factors such as
ignorance, inexperience, lack of communication, and
ineptness; such practitioners would not consider frigidity
as globally as would a psychoanalyst. Instead, they would
isolate it and break it down into discrete entities (Gagnon,
1977, pp. 365–381; Leiblum & Pervin, 1980). In contrast, a
Freudian like Helene Deutsch interpreted frigidity as an
outgrowth of basic psychological blockage. Psychoanalysis held as a matter of principle that the alleviation
of any individual symptom was less important than a
fundamental change in character. A successfully treated
problem could, in theory, simply be replaced by a sub-

stitute. Yet when it came in practice to handling fundamental sexual dysfunctions, Freud and his immediate
circle could be clinically down-to-earth. He is known, for
example, to have prescribed contraceptives for the sake of
providing more pleasure, and not to have ignored details
connected with something as important as potency.

Whereas men can have a split in their emotional lives,
so that sex and love are separated, Helene Deutsch proposed that women suffered from a different dilemma.
Under the prevailing 'cultural conditions', she held that
women had difficulty maintaining desire where they could
not love. All this needs to be considered in the light of
Freud's contributions to the theory of love and his distinctions between masculine and feminine modes of loving.

Throughout the history of psychoanalysis, the
therapeutic bias of an individualistic and rationalist
treatment procedure has affected its theory. (One has only
to think of the early use of surrogate sex partners by
Masters and Johnson to dramatize the contrast between
the psychoanalytic 'talking cure' and one phase of sex
therapy.) Helene Deutsch may have drawn too sharp a
distinction between female and male development[1]—she
wrote, for example, that a woman's failure in the mother–
child relationship could mean frigidity, but she might well
have emphasized that if a woman treated a man as if he
were merely a child, this could be infantilizing for him and
lead, in turn, to frigidity.

Thus we see that the assumption by the vagina of
primacy in the sexual function is associated with a
maternal libidinal attitude on the woman's part.
That does not mean that a disturbance of libidinal
behaviour and its expression in frigidity involves disturbance of the reproductive function. On the contrary, we

know that there are various kinds of frigidity in which reproductive function is undisturbed, and that sterility can occur when there is full sexual sensitivity. But frigidity and sterility often go together.

Also, modern gynaecology is beginning to recognize the great importance of psychic factors in the organic course of reproduction. Recently the view has actually been expressed in gynaecological circles that in many cases sterility is a consequence of frigidity; it has been claimed that the lack of orgastic secretory discharges due to it leads to stoppages and exudations, which then form the organic substratum for sterility and somatic affections of the sexual apparatus (Kehrer, 1922).

Though this relationship between frigidity and sterility may be correct in many cases, psychoanalytic experience shows that they are generally different ways of expressing the same unconscious protest against the assumption of the complete feminine position. Now one, now another symptom may serve to express the numerous psychical determinants. When—to take a crude example—a woman consciously gives herself to her husband in the sex act but at the same time for unconscious reasons refuses herself, it is to be assumed that as she refuses to receive him completely into herself she will also refuse him the child as the expected sequel of that reception and will thus remain both frigid and sterile. But it frequently occurs that the woman is frigid and yet has a number of children or, alternatively, that she achieves full orgasm and yet remains sterile without any primary organic cause. In the first instance the unconscious has failed to disturb the autonomous activity of copulation between ovum and sperm, and in the second unconscious tendencies have made the wish for children independent of relations with the sex object.

We shall return below to the many possibilities that arise here and that we have been able to observe in the analysis of dreams and symptom-formations. At all events, we have already seen that the two disturbances (frigidity and sterility) are interconnected and influence each other.

It is a very striking and psychologically still unexplained fact that frigidity among women is much more frequent than is psychic impotence, the corresponding disturbance among men. Though it is not easy to clear up the question completely, we shall at least try to contribute something to a better understanding ot it.

We must not forget that frigidity, like male impotence, should be regarded as a neurotic symptom.

The same mechanisms apply that are analytically familiar to us in symptom formation and into which we cannot go here. Thus for some of the way male impotence and female frigidity take parallel courses in this respect.

What, then, are the specific causal factors in women that result in this divergence in the frequency of appearance of the disturbance?

Freud (1910h, 1912d) has pointed out that one of the causes of male impotence is to be sought in the circumstances that certain inhibitions can develop in the libido that often lead to a split into two components: affectionate and sensual. This leads to an only qualified capacity for sexual activity, in the sense that a tenderly loved object cannot simultaneously be sensually desired, and *vice versa*. The object in relation to which sensuality can freely express itself has to be despised, debased, looked down on. This attitude can lead to impotence but gives the man much greater freedom of movement in the choice of objects for sexual intercourse. This splitting tendency, traces of which are present in all men, can have pathological results in the sense that 'where he loves he cannot desire', but it can also take the form: 'He can desire, i.e., be potent, where he does not love.' Thus favourable conditions are created for a wide range of possible sexual activity.

For the normal woman, however, these opportunities do not exist in our cultural conditions; her capacity for loving is generally expressed in the formula: 'Where she does not love, she cannot desire.'

This divergence of attitude is explained by the different nature of the reaction to the real frustration with which—as we have mentioned above in a different context—the sexually mature boy and girl are faced at the time of puberty.

The young man eventually succeeds in breaking out of the frustrations. As a consequence of the internal conflict that has already arisen out of the Oedipus complex, this breakthrough often takes place only on condition that the love object is debased, and this condition is adhered to in later love life.

This constellation does not occur in the case of the girl, who has to adhere to the ban until she makes a permitted object choice. She therefore persists longer with clitoral masturbation, accompanied by unconscious fantasies.

The object choice is then made without any split, but with a correspondingly greater limitation of choice and with a danger of incestuous fixation.

Another reason why frigidity is commoner than impotence lies in the predominance of the psychical element in the sexual life of woman. Psychoanalysis has shown us that man creates higher cultural products by the sublimation of unused sexual driving forces and thus achieves satisfaction of ego tendencies at the cost of the sexual drives. With women, things are different. Women's sublimatory capacities, perhaps quantitatively not less than those of men, are subject to different guiding principles. Productive capacity, which in man finds an outlet in his intellectual and social achievements and gives him narcissistic satisfaction, is in women confined to the narrow confines of sex life and the production of children. Everything that can give her narcissistic satisfaction is closely bound up with the sexual function. Instinctual components for which no use has been found are devoted to deepening and intensifying the psychical components of sex life. Among women all the libido that in men is withdrawn from sexuality and directed to the outside world remains centred on the sexual function. This is another factor leading to the overloading of the sensuous with the mental, making love relationships more difficult.

For further understanding of woman's greater disposition to sexual frigidity we must once again recall the difficulties of puberty that we discussed earlier. These (in contrast to the male) lie chiefly in the repressive boost to which pre-pubertal sexual activity has finally to submit. This was male-oriented and bound to the clitoris, and that part of it that was not disposed of in the repressive boost becomes a disturbing factor in the path of the full development of womanliness—a factor, moreover, that is continually reactivated by that traumatic experience of puberty, the periodic recurrence of menstruation. This not completely disposed-of clitoral phase is a frequent cause of frigidity, of refusal to adapt to the female-passive vaginal receptive role.

We have already mentioned the after-effects of pubertal prohibitions and the act of defloration and their relationship to frigidity. We also pointed out that frigidity and psychogenic sterility have the same origins as the neuroses. Like the latter, they are dependent on the intensity of infantile fixations, on the fate of the Oedipus complex, and on adherences to earlier erogenous zones, etc. In this connection it should be recalled that in woman a normally stronger cathexis of the erogenous zones than is the case in man also leads to a stronger fixation on those zones. In particular the oral zone and the nipples are reluctant to sacrifice their erogenous significance in favour of the vagina.

NOTE

1. Even recent writers still commit a similar reductionist mistake. Nancy Friday (1977), in rightly emphasizing the unique relationship of mother and daughter, excludes other factors, for example the role of fathers. After conceding that the 'mother is not the only determining factor in the girl's life', she goes on: 'But whatever else happens to us in relationships to fathers, peers, teachers—the tie to mother is the one constant, a kind of lens through which all that follows is seen' (p. 144).

CHAPTER NINE

Pregnancy and confinement

A key to understanding Freud's whole perspective is
that he saw sexuality in terms of the evolutionary value
system of procreation (Schafer, 1974). Helene Deutsch
made her basic differentiation between male and female
accordingly. In 1925 she thought of the vagina as a
potential 'duplication' of the woman's self and talked
about how the penis could 'develop into an erogenous
zone before the development of its sexual function' (see
chapters five and six). In her view, to the woman the act
of parturition becomes the conclusion of the sex act
begun in coitus. Through using Freud's speculations
about the existence of a death instinct, she could try to
account for the neurotic fears and forebodings associated
with childbirth, as well as certain graver but well-
known post-partum difficulties. For the woman pregnancy itself represents a special emotional upheaval,
and subsequent literature has followed up Helene
Deutsch's early suggestions: it is now considered a nor-

79

mal 'maturational' phase (Bibring et al., 1961). The birth of an infant, she had held, brings about in a woman 'a change in the whole attitude towards life'. The woman's relation to the child not only continues the bond to her sexual partner but also revives the love for her father. The newborn child is at the same time the recipient of its mother's ambivalences. Helene Deutsch thought that signs of these hostile trends, reactivated earlier phases, could be detected in some of the earliest symptoms of pregnancy; but today it is widely held that these problems can be reduced if women 'can count on their husband's care and loving participation in their great experience' (Benedek, 1959, p. 739).

In keeping with the state of psychoanalytic thinking of the time, Helene Deutsch excluded the role of a woman's relationship to her own mother during this period of exceptional stress. But she was ahead of her time in explaining the special preciousness of a child to its mother. The child can be such an immense gratification to a woman because it embodies her ego ideal, in a way that—since it is 'biologically prefigured'—can never be exactly matched for a man. To the woman 'everything that is considered psychically valuable, worth aspiring to, and innocent is now materialized in the child'.

Parental disappointments are inevitable. And from the outset of the child's birth the unity with its mother cannot be completely peaceable. Without ignoring the large part that 'physical factors, actual living conditions, etc.' play, Helene Deutsch concentrated on the independent role of psychological conflicts. While some women would never become full people without reproducing themselves and reach physical and psychical prime in pregnancy, others suffer as an 'uncomfortable appendix' of their child. Helene Deutsch, although a pathfinder within psychoanalysis and psychiatry, did not discuss the possibility that some women might be better off not bearing children.

With the act of introjection the reproductive function of the male comes to an end; it is completed with the relief of sexual tension that goes with ejaculation.

This one-act junction is in the case of the female divided into two. The first of these, however, that of incorporation, contains elements that point to a tendency to get rid of the germ plasm in coitus by expulsion, just as in the case of the males. In addition to identification with the male, female orgasm seems also to have a causal function, expressing an attempt to give coitus a birth-giving quality, making it a 'missed labour', let us say. This process of ejecting the product of reproduction in the act of mating is also very frequent among females in the animal kingdom.

In the human female this process, which is not carried out but is obviously hinted at and begun in orgasm, is concluded in the second act, that of parturition. Thus we have here a process that is divided into two phases only by a time interval. Just as the first act contains an element of the second (in orgasm), so the second is impregnated with pleasure mechanisms of the first. I even believe that the act of birth represents the acme of sexual pleasure through relief of the tension of the irritant effect of the germ plasm. The act of parturition would then be an 'automatic process', like ejaculation (according to Ferenczi, 1938), which requires the intensive stimulus of the ripened embryo to begin functioning. The view that Groddeck first courageously put forward at The Hague Congress, that the act of parturition is associated with pleasure because of its resemblance to coitus, would then need to be amended to the proposition that coitus is a pleasurable act chiefly because of the psychological fact that it represents an attempt at and a beginning of the act of parturition. In support of this view I should like to put forward the following:

We know from Freud that the sadistic destructive drive reaches its highest expression when the sexual drives emanating from Eros are eliminated. This is the case after they have attained relief in the act of obtaining sexual satisfaction. The death drive then has a free hand and can assert its demands unhindered. A classic example of this is provided by the lower animals, among whom the sex act leads to death.

This applies to the fertilizing male, but in my view it is also repeated *mutatis mutandis* in the female, when the fertilized egg is ejected after a longer or shorter period of maturation in the maternal body. In a number of species—among certain spiders, for instance—the female perishes after the conclusion of the reproductive process. If the liberation of the death wish is a consequence of the satisfaction of sexual trends, logically one can only assume that in the case of the female this reaches its peak in the act of parturition.

In fact, the act of parturition is an orgy of masochistic pleasure for the female, and the fears and forebodings of death that precede it are clearly a presentiment of the threat represented by the destructive drives about to be released.

States of confusion that often set in after confinement are marked by an especially strong tendency to suicide or impulses to kill the newborn infant.

I find confirmation in these facts for my theory that to the woman the act of parturition represents the conclusion of the sex act that began in coitus, and that, as with the male, the final satisfaction of Eros goes hand in hand with a simultaneous separation of soma and germ plasm.

The interval between the two acts is filled with complicated processes in the libidinal economy. We have learned from a number of studies in recent years (by Ferenczi, Groddeck, Felix Deutsch) that organic illnesses involve disturbance of the normal distribution of the libido, that organic damage produces changes of libidinal position, and that quantities of libido are released and bound again in the process. Further investigation of what happens to the libido in organic illnesses will no doubt lead to many new discoveries.

Pregnancy

In this connection there arises the question of what specific psychological processes arise in pregnancy. The condition is of course 'physiological' but causes such an upheaval in normal somatic behaviour with regard to metabolism, circulation of the blood, dislocation of organs, changes of function, and new demands on the physique that the mere fact of the parallelism of physical and mental phenomena should long since have suggested the question of what happens to the psychic apparatus in relation to all this. Also, we must not overlook the fact that this condition involves new object relations and that the appearance on the scene of a new real object—the child—brings about a change in the whole attitude to life.

We mentioned above that the advent of sexual maturity in women is marked by a narcissistic wound. We observed that the subsequent processes of periodically recurring menstruation, and then the act of defloration, always represent a trauma in the sense of wounded narcissism, and we saw the way in which the hurt ego sought to compensate itself for the inroads of the reproductive function. A child was promised the female ego as a reward and compensation for what it had undergone.

How, then, does the female ego react to the wish-fulfilment when it has taken place? How are the narcissistic wounds wiped out?

We have followed woman's progress from the attainment of sexual maturity, and we regarded the course of development up to that time as bisexual, i.e., common to male and female. At this point we must take another backward glance at that infantile—let us call it 'pre-female'—period, since we know that all phases of development leave traces in the unconscious that are reactivated at suitable moments.

Analytic experience has shown that childish curiosity is intensely concerned with the question of reproduction. The child's fantasy is full of theories that arise in spite of attempted false explanations by adults; in fact, the tendency to fabricate these products of fantasy is so strong in the child that they arise even when the correct sexual explanation has not been withheld. Many of these theories are so typical, recur so obstinately in the dream structures of all mankind, and make such a constant contribution to the formation of neurotic symptoms and recur so regularly in different forms of sublimation that we are justified in counting them among the permanent contents of the unconscious. One of these typical fantasies is that of oral fertilization, and another is that of the 'anal child'. The latter is further supplemented by the equation faeces = penis = child, all of which is determined in a number of directions (Freud, 1917c, p. 127). The equation child = penis offers the woman a child as a direct substitute for the penis missed in the castration complex. Here we should like briefly to point out the connection of these fantasies with actual phylogenetic forms of development. For among lower animals we in fact find processes in which the close connection between the mouth and genital apparatus is plain; similarly, the connection between the genital function and excretory processes is extremely frequent. Both are forms that find frequent expression in ontogenetic development. Both infantile fantasies, that of the oral and that of the anal origin of the child, are for their part closely connected with the corresponding pre-genital phases of development of the libido (see above). It seems to us to be of psychological interest to enquire whether these infantile fallacies are mobilized in any form in the real situation of reproduction (having established that they have betrayed their persistence elsewhere after being stored in the unconscious). We know that in men these unconscious contents of the mind lead to intellectual and social activity and that in women they are interwoven with the reproductive function.

Thus in coitus, which to woman (psychologically) represents the beginning of reproductive activity, place is found for accommodating lower positions of the libido. As we

have seen, there is an introduction of the sexual partner—an incorporation of a part of him through the agency
of the genital secretion. There is a far-reaching analogy
between this incorporation and the sucking activity of the
infant who 'incorporates' part of the mother's body by
means of a fluid that it extracts. The analogy is complete.
In the act of sexual preparation the separation between ego
and object is completely eliminated; true, the object exists
in the outside world, but, as in the case of the infant at the
breast, the antithesis between ego and mother does not
exist, since the breast becomes part of the infant's body;
similarly in the ecstasy of the sex act the antithesis
between ego and object also ceases to exist. Here the penis
assumes the intermediary role as the organ of sucking,
while the vagina as the sucking organ takes over the oral
function. In this transfer of oral activity to the vagina the
infantile theory of oral fertilization finds its home. The
perversion of fellatio is the pathological expression of this
state of affairs.

Thus coitus represents that completely harmonious state
in which identity between subject and object has been
restored. The real incorporation of the object takes place in
the act of fertilization and is continued in the child, to
which the role of incorporated object is transferred; henceforward the relationship between subject and object is
played out between mother and child.

The introjected object, the child, is now taken up into the
woman's ego to be expanded and enriched.

The process, as we shall see below, is complicated by a
number of factors.

On the one hand, the child as an object is taken up into
the ego by way of identification and thus becomes a
component of the latter, so that part of the relationship
between mother and child establishes itself in the ego.
This state of affairs also results from the fact that the
child represents part of the ego also in the physical
respect, since it really constitutes a single entity with the
maternal body.

On the other hand, even in the womb the child represents a part of the outside world to the mother and thus
becomes an object situated outside the ego, and in relation
to it the whole of the mother's object relationships in their
positive and negative emotional attitudes are repeated.
The child, as a physical continuation of the sexual partner
through the process of introjection, has become, as it were,
the partner himself. The never superseded and now
revived oedipal constellation causes the child to become
the object of its mother's love of her father; thus the sexually mature woman's wish for a child, now fulfilled, is an
extension of her infantile desire to be given a child by her
father.

Throughout her life this attitude of the mother to her
child comes out in particular in her relationship with her
eldest son, who is destined to repeat all the qualities of his
maternal grandfather as once seen through his mother's
over-valuing child's eyes. According to statements by students of family history, there is in fact generally also a
physical resemblance between an eldest son and his maternal grandfather.[1] Thus in this object relationship the child
becomes the agent of a high human ideal in accordance
with the formula: 'You shall be like my father was.' But
analytic investigation of pregnant women has shown us
that these object relations to the child are not so simple
either. Not only is the whole of the love that was once
directed towards the father and in favourable cases to the
sexual partner too, by means of the identification described
above, extended now also to the child, but the hostile emotional attitudes to these two objects are also transferred to
the newborn child. One of the causes of this ambivalence of
feeling was the refusal of her father's love that the small
girl once experienced. The hostility that persisted in the
unconscious but was covered over by fondness was transferred simultaneously with the positive feelings to the
later love object, in relation to whom they could again be
reinforced and mobilized by subsequent experiences (the
act of defloration).

These hostile relations to objects are especially liable to come to light in the unconscious trends of pregnancy and are corrected only later in relation to the living child. They are also reinforced from other sources.

The whole conflict of ambivalence connected with the oral phases of development (see above) is contained in the process of incorporation we described earlier. This conflict is expressed in the feeling that the object that has been incorporated into the body must be expelled again. In this phase of development this tendency to expel manifests itself orally. It appears above all in morning sickness and many remarkable oral manifestations, especially in the first half of pregnancy. These manifestations include the various 'cravings', such as the characteristic hunger alternating with complete loss of appetite, or stomach-aches that cannot be explained on physical grounds alone. Study of the dreams, fantasies and above all the psychically conditioned physical sensations of pregnant women enables us to see that the old familiar equation of penis = child has been revived and has received a special reinforcement. The old identification once established by infantile sexual curiosity between the content of the bowels and the child is now reinforced by the real situation of the child in the body—a physical object that is nevertheless (like faeces and the penis in the castration complex) destined to be separated from it. Also, the oral incorporation of the child in the sex act described above determines its identity with faeces, the content of which is orally introduced in food.

Earlier we tried to show that the attainment of the highest level of libidinal organization (the vaginal phase) goes hand in hand with an intensive mobilization of regressive trends. The total liberation from the attitude of ambivalence to the object that comes about in the identificatory act of coitus is really a repetition of a situation that has already occurred in the course of development, that is, in the unification of subject and object that takes place in the infant's act of sucking. Thus the highest level of libidinal development repeats the lowest, i.e., oral level, which is characterized by identification with the object (Abraham, 1945).

In the tremendous disturbance of the libidinal economy that takes place in pregnancy the path of regression once entered upon leads to all abandoned libidinal trends being sought out.

It is not only the infantile object cathexes belonging to the genital organization that are again mobilized in relation to the child. We have already discussed manifestations of regression to the oral phase, and we now see that in the equation faeces = child the genital organization undergoes yet another reduction to the sadistic-anal level.

A quantity of narcissistic libido was associated with the incorporation of the child as a part of the woman's own body (in the identification between child and ego), and in the same way the relationship originating from the identification between child and faeces is again a narcissistic one. This derives from the high valuation once attached in infancy to one's own bodily excreta. Similarly, in the identification of a child with penis the narcissistic valuation of the penis is preserved and transferred to the child.

Regression to the sadistic-anal phase is manifested not only in the fantasies and dreams of pregnancy. We also detect it in the pregnant woman's very typical temporary character changes that originate, according to analytic findings, in the sadistic-anal phase of development, e.g., stubbornness, capriciousness, particular cleanliness, thrift bordering on meanness, and a kind of collecting mania. These characteristics can all be rationalized as concern for the child that is going to be born.

The attitude of ambivalence to the object peculiar to the sadistic-anal phase also manifests itself in numerous symptoms of pregnancy. The symptoms of labour that often appear long before confinement without physical cause are a manifestation of the expulsion trends of this ambivalent attitude to the child. If these negative trends predominate, they can lead to a miscarriage.

A number of complaints associated with pregnancy are connected with the anal phase. Thus the morning sickness we mentioned above is often an expression of typical feelings of disgust. We know that to the child excreta are cathected with disgust in reaction to the original narcissistic over-valuation of them, and that they thus become the very essence of the unclean and the disgusting. The pregnant woman's disgust, whether as a general sensation or directed at food she normally likes, are also related to the unconscious connection between child and faeces.

It is generally known that with the beginning of the child's movements in the fifth month of pregnancy all these sensations disappear. Psychologically this fact is determined in two ways. In the first place, the child's independent motoric activity puts it more into the outside world, and new feelings of tenderness and mother-love flow towards it as a result.

As part of its mother's body but nevertheless equipped with a certain movement and independence of its own, the child loses its anal significance; also, the narcissistic component of the libido attached to it moves to a higher level of development—is genitalized. The child is equated to the penis and in that capacity takes over the task of compensating the woman for her loss of the penis.

The relationship to the child, still embedded in the deepest narcissism, is now brought to a higher level of development—the phallic. At the same time the child, by the development of a certain independence that now manifests itself, demonstrates that it belongs to the outside world and thus begins to take its place among the mother's object relationships. The conflict of ambivalence seems to be eased by this, the ejection tendency is lessened, the child can be kept. Thus we see that object relations with the child exist simultaneously and side by side with these purely narcissistic relations and that even in the womb it also has the meaning of an object in the outside world and becomes a libidinal repository for various object cathexes.

Let us follow for a moment its further destiny in the purely narcissistic respect.

The object–child introjected in the sex act becomes a component of the woman's own ego. In the process of introjection the quantities of libido flowing to the partner in the sex act are transformed into narcissistic libido. These quantities are very considerable, for, as we have seen, they contain a large amount of maternal libido, and above all, libido directed at the father. This libido flowing to the ego represents the woman's 'secondary' narcissism in that, though it is directed at the child–object, the object at the same time represents part of the ego.

The ego change that takes place in the pregnant woman as a result of the process of introjection is a new edition of a process that has taken place before: to the woman the child becomes an incarnation of her previously developed ego-ideal. This is set up for a second time through introjection of the father.

The narcissistic libido is transferred to this newly established superego, to which are attributed all the perfect qualities that were once attributed to the father. A whole mass of libidinal object cathexes are withdrawn from the outside world and attributed to the child as superego. The sublimatory process in women is thus related to the child.

While men measure and check their ego ideal against their works of sublimation in the outside world, women's ego ideal is embodied in the child, and all the sublimatory trends that men use for their intellectual and social activity in the case of women flow to the child as their work of sublimation (in the psychological sense).

Freud has seen the relationship of parents to their children as the highest of all manifestations of narcissistic love. But in men this relationship never attains the same intensity as it does in women, in whom it is, so to speak, biologically prefigured. For the child arises in her own ego by way of introjection, and large quantities of narcissistic libido flow to it before it becomes an object. Later the par-

ents' unfulfilled wishes are centred on the child, which has
the task of compensating them for the disappointments
they have suffered. The earliest relationship between
mother and child, in which the child still represents a part
of the maternal ego, is already under the aegis of this. As
we have seen, in this relationship the child corresponds to
that part of the ego that represents the woman's ego-ideal.
Everything that is considered psychically valuable, worth
aspiring to, and innocent is now materialized in the child.

The perfect harmony in which there is no dividing line
between subject and object (see above), which was first
obtained with the partner in the sex act is continued with
the child, and thus the mother–child relationship represents a complete realization of the primary condition in
which there was not yet any separation between ego libido
and object libido.

However, this primary condition is disturbed by two factors:

1. By a process of sublimation the child becomes the
   mother's superego, which—as we have found in other
   contexts—can come into sharp conflict with the
   maternal ego.

2. The child is at the same time an object in the outside
   world on which the conflicts of ambivalence of all
   phases of development of the libido are played out.

Observation of the psychic changes brought about by
pregnancy shows that the reactions are manifold and very
individual. That on the one hand physical factors, actual
living conditions, etc., play a big part cannot be denied. On
the other hand, the great upheaval in the libidinal economy is bound to involve reactions that are independent of
actuality. Analytic observation has confirmed conjecture
that dispositional factors that have never been manifested
in normal circumstances are now reactivated. When these
are present in excessive strength, they lead to the outbreak
of psychic illnesses (pregnancy psychoses, puerperal and

lactation psychoses, etc.). In normal cases they lead to certain change of psychical disposition still within the limits of the physiological.

Observation has shown us that there are two characteristic types of women insofar as their psychical reactions to pregnancy are concerned. Many women react to pregnancy with evident discomfort and depression, and this is accompanied by an unfavourable change in physical disposition; they become unattractive and actually shrink, so that with the progressive development of the child they in fact change into an uncomfortable appendix of the latter. The other type of woman attains physical and psychical prime in pregnancy.

In the case of the first type, the woman's narcissism has suffered a loss in favour of the child; on the one hand the superego has taken complete charge of the ego, and on the other the child as love object has attracted to itself such a large amount of ego libido that the ego has been impoverished. Perhaps that is the explanation of the melancholia of pregnancy.

In the other type of woman the distribution of libido in pregnancy takes place differently. The part of the libido that is now withdrawn from the outside world is transferred to the child as a component part of the ego. This takes place only if the formation of the superego is less intense and the child is regarded less as an object and more as a component of the ego; in this event there is an increase of secondary narcissism that manifests itself in increased self-feeling, self-satisfaction, etc.

From what we have said, it will be seen that the unity of mother and child is not so completely peaceable as it may seem.

The initial harmony of the primary condition that began with the process of introjection of the sex act is soon disturbed by the ambivalent phenomena that take place in relation to the child in the womb. In the light of this insight the act of delivery presents itself to us as the final result of a long, furious struggle. The stimulus proceeding

from the foetus becomes intolerable and presses for discharge. In this final struggle all the hostile impulses that
have been mobilized in the course of the pregnancy reach
their greatest intensity. In the physical respect this struggle manifests itself in the contracting activity of the mus-
culature and its tendencies to retain and to expel. The
latter finally gain the upper hand. The introjected object is
projected into the outside world, and by the route by which
it was introjected in coitus.

We have seen that in the ego unity that was established
the introjected object assumed the place of the ego-ideal.
Projected into the outside world it retains this quality, in
that it continues to represent an embodiment of the
mother's own unfulfilled ideals. This is the psychological
path by which, as Freud says, woman advances 'from narcissism to full object love'.

This mother–child identity enables us to draw conclusions about the psychical state of the child during birth
from the psychical condition of the woman. The former—
which succumbs to amnesia—is later only dimly remembered in dream formations and fantasies.

To the woman it is as if the world were coming apart
and sinking; there is a chaotic sense of being utterly lost, a
feeling of pressure and of bursting transferred from the
genital passages to the head, combined with an intense
fear of death. No doubt it is a complete repetition of the
fear associated with the trauma of birth and the conquest
of that fear by the real act of reproduction. What the man
seeks in coitus and what drives him on to laborious sublimations is attained by woman in the function of reproduction.

It is well known that pregnant women frequently dream
of a swimming child. The latter is always identifiable as
the dreamer herself, equipped with a quality that makes
her, or in her childhood made her, especially valuable in
her own eyes—proof and illustration, as it were, of the formation of the ego-ideal in the child. The birth fantasies of
women who have themselves given birth turn out on suffi-

cient investigation to represent the details of two acts of birth woven into one. They are a condensation of their own—never remembered—birth and of their confinement.

NOTE

1. There is a belief among many primitive tribes that grandfathers are reborn in a maternal grandson. For an analysis of this belief see Reik (1914).

CHAPTER TEN

The psychology of childbed

In accord with some of the most recent arguments on behalf of natural childbirth, Helene Deutsch proposed that the use of drugs to diminish birth pangs had unfavourable psychological results. Although narcosis may eliminate the phase of 'emptiness and disappointment', it also entails feelings of strangeness; she thought it had the consequence that 'the joyful new attitude to the child is not so ecstatic and not so surprising in its intensity as it is when birth takes its natural course'. It is partly due to an appreciation of psychodynamic factors that the use of general anaesthesia in labour has been restricted to surgical procedures, or as a last resort.

Although Helene Deutsch did not touch on the man's possible feminine wishes, she was aware how the woman's relationship to her husband, in terms of her inner life, is necessarily complicated by the act of having given birth. Children do seem to involve a woman's sexual disengagement from her husband. The young child can become a competitor of hers, just at the time when

95

her own maternal feelings are being withdrawn from her mate towards their infant. In her weakened state, and out of identification with her newborn, she may feel child-like herself. But Helene Deutsch did not under-estimate the impact of specifically chemical forces, especially in helping to account for psychosis.

The psychic state of women after confinement is under the aegis of several different trends.

At first there is the tremendous relief of a tri-umphantly ended struggle. This is followed by a very brief stage of infinite emptiness and disappointment. This stage generally succumbs to amnesia and in most cases can be brought to light again only by women with an exceptional gift for introspective observation. This feeling is the supreme manifestation of the narcissistic wound we met in other contexts as the reaction of disappointment at having 'no child and no penis'. It is a loss of the libidinal position associ-ated with the child's having been part of the woman's body; the ego has suffered a loss, the woman's body has suffered a diminution, there has been another castration in that the child was equated with the penis.

The void is filled only when a definitive relationship with the child as an object in the outside world is estab-lished and a portion of the previously narcissistic libido is transferred to this new object. When the reproductive pro-cess takes a normal and favourable course, the woman does, indeed, find in the bliss of this new acquisition a com-pensation for earlier afflications.

Among women who try to diminish the final birth pangs through narcosis, confinement takes a very characteristic course. The phase of emptiness and disappointment is lack-ing, but against that the joyful new attitude to the child is not so ecstatic and not so surprising in its intensity as it is when birth takes its natural course.

This 'last moment of disappointment' is evidently necessary to enable the pleasure of the 'compensation' to be fully
felt. Also, it is the final moment of delivery of the head
that completes the analogy to coitus (*immissio penis*) (see,
for example, Rank, 1929). In the vaginal passage there is a
border-line at which the child for the last time represents a
part of the woman's own body, while at the same time it
has become an expelled object. Thus there is a repetition of
the moment in the sex act when the object was still felt to
be a piece of the outside world but was at the same time
being introjected and was on the border between the outside world and the self. Thus the completion of the object
relationship with the child that began in the womb is manifested in the genital passages, and the bridge to this relationship is finally and completely established in the
pleasurable masochistic experience of pain. When this is
missed, the child is at first received with a feeling of
strangeness.

The influence that pregnancy has on a woman's psyche
has a sequel in childbed. In the first place a readjustment
is necessitated by the fact that the child is no longer part of
the maternal body but has completely become an object in
the outside world. The consequence of this is that the portion of libido that was directed at the child during pregnancy as part of the maternal ego loses its narcissistic
cathexis and presses for new employment. Secondly, there
is the further complication resulting from the fact that the
child has also become an independent being for other persons who have emotional relationships with the mother
and often appears as a competitor of hers.

The woman's relationship to her husband is complicated
above all by the fact that a large part of the libidinal ties
that resulted from her maternal attitude to him are now
transferred from him to the child. As a consequence of her
state of physical and psychical weakness, but primarily as
a consequence of her identification with the newborn, the
woman herself becomes a child and feels diminished in her

position as centre of interest on whom once upon a time in her own childhood all the affection and concern of the environment had been lavished.

The ambivalent attitude to the child that manifested itself during pregnancy was suppressed by the narcissistic valuation of the child as identical with her own ego, but now that the unity has been broken up, it gains in intensity.

There is evidently also a far-reaching correlation between the hormonal and chemical processes that exercise a strong general influence on the body during pregnancy and the psychical changes we have described.

In particular, their contribution to the development of the psychoses of pregnancy must not be underrated, above all in regard to the states of confusion that often appear as reactions to toxic noxae. The psychic shock of the confinement and the subsequent necessity of libidinal change, as well as circulatory changes and changes in the processes of metabolism, combined with additional factors such as infection, etc., often lead to psychotic states. It is characteristic, though readily intelligible from the attitude to the newborn child that we have described above, that the aggressiveness that appears in this state of excitation is often turned against the child and can, if there is insufficient supervision, even lead to the killing of the child. In the absence of inhibitions components of hatred that lurk behind the really existing mother-love break through.

CHAPTER ELEVEN

Lactation

According to Helene Deutsch, breast-feeding was subject to all the insecurities and anxieties associated with a woman's sense of femaleness. She even compared an analytically observed disturbance of lactation with premature ejaculation in a man.

At a time when sexual roles, at least in connection with the rearing of infants, were more sharply differentiated than they are apt to be in middle-class circles today, Helene Deutsch did not need to touch on how left-out the husband may come to feel. One ought not to forget how much early psychoanalytic thinking presupposed the ready availability of servants. Even as the abolition of some traditional sex differences becomes possible, the technology of periodic bottle-feeding can still threaten the mother with interferences in her flow of milk. Modern circumstances, with new demands on men, have made it possible for the husband to be left frustrated and jealous about the greater intimacy between mother and child.

The pain of physical separation from the child is extinguished when it is first put to the breast. The mother–child unit is re-established, and the process of incorporation, which in the sex act took place through the vagina, making use of the oral sucking mechanisms, and which was continued in pregnancy, now undergoes a repetition—with a reversal of roles between the two partners in the sucking act. The complete psychological analogy of both sucking situations, i.e., in coitus and in lactation, arises above all from the circumstance that in both the boundary between subject and object is wiped out, and also from the identity of the oral incorporation of the object in the act of sucking. Once more there is an equation between penis and nipple. As the penis took control of the vagina in coitus and created an erogenous centre in the act of doing so, so does the erect mammary gland now take control of the infant's mouth. Just as the erogeneity of the whole body then flowed to the vagina, so does the whole disseminated libido of the newborn child flow to its mouth. The part of the seminal fluid is here played by the flow of milk. The identification established in infantile fantasy between maternal breast and paternal penis is now realized for the second time; in coitus the penis took over the role of the mammary gland, and in the act of lactation the mammary gland becomes the penis. In the situation of identification the boundary between the partners disappears—and in this mother–child relationship the mother once again wipes out the trauma of weaning.

A remarkable disturbance of breast-feeding that I was able to observe analytically made the identification between penis and breast especially clear to me. A young mother with a very ambivalent relationship to her child had to give up breast-feeding even though she wished to continue with it and possessed an amply functioning mammary apparatus. What happened was that in the interval between the child's feeding times the milk came gushing out, with the result that the breast was empty when the child was put to it. The practices to which she resorted to circumvent this unhappy state of affairs recalled the behaviour of a man suffering from premature ejaculation who desperately tries to accelerate the sex act but is always overtaken with the same lack of success—she was invariably too late. Analysis of the disturbance took us back to its urethral origin in her case too. A more frequent disturbance of lactation—the drying up of the secretion—is unmistakably dominated by other (anal) components of the process.

We have known for a long time that there is a close correlation between processes connected with the genitals and with the breast, both in the psychological and the hormonal respect.

This reciprocal independence is manifested in a variety of ways. Thus stimulation of the nipples not only produces reactions in the stimulated organ; states of intense excitation of the genitals going all the way to orgasm can be attained by this route. It is well known that when a baby is first put to the breast, there can be more or less intense contractions of the uterus, and that genital processes greatly influence lactation.

One of the oldest psychoanalytic discoveries was that the earliest level of organization in the course of human sexual development is the oral level, associated with the infant's feeding activity. Its sucking activity, in addition to satisfying the instinct of self-preservation, simultaneously represents a libidinal action.

In the mother–child unit the female breast in the act of suckling also plays the part of an organ of sexual satisfaction. The mother's great pleasure does not lie only in the act of feeding and the thriving of the child; it is also an act of sexual enjoyment, at the heart of which the mammary gland plays the part of an erogenous zone. This 'erotogeneity' of the mammary gland frequently leads to feeding difficulties, the psychogenous nature of which is still often not recognized. As soon as an over-emphasis of the sexual role of the sucking apparatus appears, repression sets in. But repression of the libidinal aspect can also involve other components of the feeding function, and so these are denied too, resulting in an inability to suckle that often cannot be influenced by any means whatsoever.

The variations of the secretional activity of the mammary glands under the influence of psychical factors are well known. But what is not recognized is that the chief reasons lie in the unconscious, and that a repetition is taking place during lactation of conflicts that have already occurred during pregnancy. The whole conflict of ambivalence between giving and refusing, emptying and drying up, takes place once more without the mother in her desperate struggles about her suckling ability having any suspicion that the disturbances arise from her hostile attitudes to her beloved child.

In favourable cases the negative trends are successfully overcome by positive ones, until the unity is finally broken up by the sadistic impulses of the child, manifesting itself in biting the maternal breast.

CHAPTER TWELVE

The menopause

In well-meaning efforts to redress the imbalance inherent in Freud's own views about women, contemporary writers are sometimes in the danger of going too far in denying the inevitability of differences between the sexes.[1] It is odd that, in contrast to *Psychoanalysis of the Sexual Functions of Women,* so much theoretical effort since then has sought to undermine the inevitability of bisexuality (see, for example, Kardiner, Karush, & Ovesey, 1959; Rado, 1940). Of course the word 'bisexual' has historically been used in a wide variety of contexts, from foetal development to manifest homosexual behaviour; and it may have been used for authoritarian clinical purposes. Fortunately, few informed psychoanalysts have tended to stigmatize bisexuality in women as a 'phallic fixation' (Benedek, 1959, pp. 729–730), or a consequence of the wish to reject femininity.

In terms of the broadest meaning of the concept of bisexuality, however, the early Freudians were, like the Bloomsbury literary group in England (Bell, 1972;

Holroyd, 1967–68), trying to criticize previous preconceptions about femininity and masculinity. For each
human to be both male and female allows for the rich-
ness of multiple possibilities and peculiarities. At its
best, psychoanalysis ought to represent a challenge to
any society's prevailing conventions.

In the act of trying to assert the moral equality of
women, writers may willy-nilly have involved psychoanalysis in new conformist uses. To the degree that
people are creatures of social forces, it is, in my view,
necessary to abandon the possible hope of instincts
remaining at odds with culture for the sake of human
autonomy. Evidence for developmental differences in the
sexes persists and ought to be morally welcome. We now
know, for example, that in terms of the rate of cerebral
lateralization, the left hemisphere matures earlier in
girls than in boys. Any generalizations are bound to
have their drawbacks; but if we have only begun to
understand what might conceivably be innately feminine or masculine, and the role society can play, it
would be perverse in terms of human freedom to try to
obliterate the distinctions between the sexes. Furthermore, the concept of psychological 'normality' is in itself
an ethically questionable one, and Freud and his early
followers could rightly be sceptical about the value of
'health'.

Malfunctioning is of course easier to discuss; even
though the existence of a male climacteric, to which
Helene Deutsch alludes here, is now widely acknowledged, menopause is still bound to have special mean-
ings for a woman. In her view it is the last feminine
sexual ordeal.

Freudian theory is often held to be unduly alarmist
and pessimistic, more so than revisionist ideas which
stress the role of social forces in shaping personality
development. Yet on the subject of menopause it may be
that Helene Deutsch's early approach was not ade-
quately appreciative of the full extent of this develop-

mental crisis for a woman; perhaps her theory, which emphasizes the regressive repetition of pubertal conflicts in menopause, lagged behind her clinical judgement. Adolescence involves an enormous boost in ovarian hormones; but what gives way in menopause is not just a woman's reproductive capacities, but some of the feminine primacy of earliest years. What can be so frightening about this phase is that it is not so much an 'epilogue' of something that has occurred before, but rather the creation of a new state of affairs that has never existed before.

The 'post-genital' period was, in Helene Deutsch's view, a second time in which, from an evolutional perspective, male and female no longer exist. Yet her case material, which she allows herself to use here, illustrates the special consequences for the woman of this particular upheaval in life. She notes the narcissistically determined increase of libido, as well as the heightened need to be desired and loved. A woman's life, however, does not by any means have to be restricted to issues connected with child-bearing, especially given the 'biologically revived bisexual constitution.'

Helene Deutsch pointed out some unique possibilities for sublimation that arise after the end of menstruation. She concludes her book on an altogether optimistic note about the efficacy of psychoanalysis as prophylaxis, which was in accord with the hopes of her new profession in the 1920s. Later clinical scepticism weakened her initial enthusiasm. But one of the attractions of psychoanalysis, a surrogate religion for some of its early practitioners, was its optimism about the chances of transforming human fate. With the faith that knowledge ultimately means power, and in the conviction that how we think affects our behaviour, she had singled out femininity to be her speciality. Whatever the inevitable limitations to Helen Deutsch's pioneering ideas, her work stands as one memorable account of the complexities in a woman's development.

W e have now followed the development of the sexual life of women from the attainment of sexual maturity to the complete fulfilment of the function of reproduction. As far as the infantile prehistory of these phases of development is concerned, we have drawn attention only to those factors that seemed to us to be absolutely essential to an understanding of the whole process.

Woman's last traumatic experience as a sexual being, the menopause, is under the aegis of an incurable narcissistic wound. In complete parallel to the physical process, this represents a retrogressive phase in the history of the libido, a regression to abandoned, infantile libidinal positions.

The real frustrations of this period of life, which do not run parallel with the disappearance of libidinal needs, create a psychical situation coping with which is a task that makes great psychological demands.

We have seen how the girl's real frustrations at the age of puberty are compensated for, and how the narcissistic wound of the final renunciation of masculinity is wiped out by the appearance of secondary sexual characteristics and a new feminine physical attractiveness.

At the menopause everything that was granted the feminine being at puberty is taken back. Simultaneously with the processes of genital retrogression the beautifying activity of internal glandular secretions ceases, and the secondary sexual characteristics come under the aegis of the loss of femininity.

The libido, now without the possibility of cathexis and with a diminished capacity for sublimation, has to go into reverse and seek out earlier positions, i.e., set out on the path that is familiar to us from the formation of neurotic symptoms.

It is to be assumed that the genitals do not give up their function easily or without a long and difficult struggle. For every phase of development of the libido has the tendency to retain its cathexis, and this persistence manifests itself after the abandonment of a level of development by exercising a lasting fascination by means of which it eases the path of libidinal regression. The persistence of lower stages of development is also no doubt the factor that makes it possible for the dismantling of the libido at the climacteric, or let us call it the post-genital, phase to take the form of clearing the way towards earlier phases.

There has been little analytic investigation of how this physiological regression takes place, of how and when it begins, of what struggles the genital libido goes through before it allows itself to be dethroned. My experiences, which I shall try to communicate here, concern only the female age of involution, and I am not in a position to make any comparisons or draw parallels with the male climacteric. But I have the impression that the psychological process in women diverges greatly from that in men, for the biological developments are completely different and more complicated and make more demands both organically and psychically on the capacity to change and adapt. What lies beyond the menopause, the complete withdrawal of libido from the genitals, is also identical in its essential features with the infantile phases of sexuality in that for the second time male and female do not exist. But before this withdrawal of libido from the genitals has been completed, before the final entry of the post-genital phase, a struggle takes place to defend the fortress that is going to be lost, and the phase of life that we call the menopause—i.e., from the middle forties to the middle fifties in the case of women—is under the aegis of that struggle. The phase is marked by certain somatic processes that are certainly causally connected with the dismantling of the genitally oriented libido in a reciprocal relationship in which it is hard to distinguish between primary and secondary factors. This difficulty arises from the fact that the biological significance of the whole process is unclear, and that it is apparently characteristic of the human female, without our seeing any analogy to it in processes either in the human male on the one hand or in the animal kingdom on the other.

In the case of the pubertal processes preparatory activity takes place in the pre-pubertal period between the ages of seven and ten, and in the same way the climacteric is preceded by a pre-climacteric at about the age of thirty, when the struggle begins.

First of all, in the organic field there is a beginning of the withdrawal of the compensations mentioned above, and in this respect an inner perception of the biological process that is taking place generally precedes the organic changes. Though still capable of conception, the woman already feels the threatened devaluation of the genitals as an organ of reproduction, and on top of this there are the external frustrations to which that function is exposed (social difficulties, etc.). The severe narcissistic blow that accompanies the process increases the narcissistic libido, and a struggle begins to preserve the acquisitions of puberty that are now beginning to vanish away. This struggle is accompanied by a reinforcement of genital trends; the increase of libido is narcissistically determined; the genitals fight to retain their position. It has often been suggested that a purely hormonal process lies behind the pre-climacteric increase in libido and that all the psychical symptoms are only consequences and concomitant phenomena of the process. The whole psychical development is certainly set off by a biological signal, just as in puberty. The difference is that while in the latter case the signal heralds a phase of construction, here it heralds a dismantling; in one case the movement is up, in the other it is down.

The later, purely regressive destiny of the libido presents the picture of a process of involution moving in the same direction as the somatic processes, and it is hard to believe that dismantling is initiated by a real intensification of the function. The latter is a purely psychical phenomenon, a reaction to dismantling processes, an overcompensation for the latter. Psychologically a complete analogy can be established between this first phase of the climacteric, which is just beginning, and the last phase of the struggles of puberty, which ended successfully with acceptance of the vagina and the object hunger streaming in from the outside world. This position of readiness, which is nevertheless subject to the 'too early' prohibition, results in a definite attitude on the girl's part during the pubertal period. The reason for this typical attitude is to be sought in the characteristic pubertal fantasies and the clitoral masturbation that is now destined to disappear but is mobilized again by the prohibition directed towards the vagina. Here we see a complete analogy between the psychical processes of the climacteric and of puberty. The part played by 'too early' in the former is played by 'too late' in the latter, and the phase in which the vaginal cathexis seeks to maintain itself is followed by that in which the libido begins its regressive decline. The impulse is provided by the progressive devaluation of the vagina in its significance as the organ of reproduction as well as failure in the outside world resulting from the greater difficulty of object finding, after which an increased libidinal hunger persists in the narcissistic need to be desired and loved. The tragi-comic result for the woman is that the older and less attractive she becomes, the greater is her desire to be loved. Under the pressure of failure the vagina gives up the struggle, and a regressive re-cathexis of the clitoris as a centre of excitation occurs, apparently in parallel with organic processes; in other words, there is a regression to the phallic phase, or to that first period of puberty in which the vagina has not yet assumed the leading role.

These two climacteric phases, both repetitions of pubertal phases in reversed order, inaugurate a photographically accurate repetition of libidinal development in regression along already foreshadowed paths. The analogy between the beginning of this regression and puberty makes clear to us the psychology of women in the early climacteric, the so-called 'dangerous age'. Let me repeat. In the first phase there is great concentration on the object, complete ability for genital realization, and predominance of a strong narcissistic desire to be loved. The second phase is characterized by vaginal disappointment, regression to clitoral masturbation, a turning away from reality, and increased fantasy activity.

These two phases, of course, flow into one another; the predominance of elements of one or the other are subject to individual variations.

At all events, typical changes of behaviour take place in which the parallels we have just established between the libido of the woman at the climacteric and the girl at puberty manifest themselves in emotional life. The renewed boost of vaginal cathexis at the first phase gives the woman a tremendous sense of uplift. She feels like a young girl, believes herself able to make a fresh start in life, as she says, feels ready for any passion, etc. She starts keeping a diary as she did when she was a girl, develops enthusiasm for some abstract idea as she did then, changes her behaviour to her family as she did before, leaves home for the same psychical reasons as girls do at puberty, etc. Her object relations change, and it is interesting to note the manifold and individually various forms taken by sexual feeling. Many women who were frigid during the reproductive period now become sexually sensitive, and others become frigid for the first time, generally in a hitherto monogamous marital relationship that can no longer satisfy their increased narcissism. Others who have hitherto put up well with frigidity now begin to demonstrate all its typical concomitant phenomena: changes of mood, unbalanced behaviour, and irritability set in and make life a torment for the woman herself and those about her.

Very characteristic is the psychical behaviour at this stage of women whose life has been under the aegis of a well-sublimated masculinity complex—I mean well-sublimated in the sense that their masculine trends have not led to neurotic derailments but have put a definite stamp on the whole of their lives. Among these women the pre-climacteric vaginal position manifests itself in the hitherto well-suppressed feminine tendencies now making their claims and coming into conflict with their masculinity complex. These women did not fall ill over the masculinity complex at puberty; they fall ill over the femininity complex at the menopause.

In pathologically distorted cases the struggle of the vagina to retain its primacy can manifest itself in extreme sexual excitation, a state of 'genital intoxication' that runs its course in the form of a hypomania. Eventually the vagina, disappointed by external failure in relation to the object and internally by incipient sterility, gives up the struggle. The libido that can no longer find a home in reality regresses to masturbatory fantasies. The libidinal relationship to the outside world succumbs to the 'too late' constellation and leads to introversion, just as the 'too early' constellation did at puberty.

The content of these fantasies, their relationship to the object, and the conversion to neurotic symptoms so completely reflects the constellation of puberty that one is continually taken aback by the unvarying consistency of the repetition principle in psychical life.

As a result of the regression of the libido from the vagina and the recathexis of the clitoris as the leading zone, the woman's whole sexuality assumes a more infantile quality; findings from the analyses of women at the climacteric show us that the task of puberty, which consisted of overcoming the Oedipus complex and masculinity complexes, never succeeds completely, even when neurosis has been successfully avoided. The reorganization of the sexual mechanism at the menopause and the transposition of the libido that goes with it is in fact only a reactivation of the struggles of puberty that were evidently never concluded. Certainly I have the impression that the menopause is more easily coped with the more successfully puberty was coped with, and that the formation of the climacteric neurosis depends on the sufficiency of the defensive arrangements made at puberty. Granted sufficient experience, it should be possible to predict the course of the menopause from the way in which puberty was coped with.

The fantasies typical of puberty, those of rape and of prostitution, are equally characteristic of the fantasizing activity of the menopause. Renewed clitoral masturbation once more mobilizes the castration complex and the anxiety and guilt feelings resulting from it. It is interesting to note that women who coped well with the castration complex in the sense of achieving womanliness, now, with the incipient retreat of the latter, once again succumb to the dominance of the castration complex and its neurotic reactions. Mobilization of this complex appears to be bound to clitoral masturbation and the anomalies of climacteric menstruation.

The above-mentioned fantasizing activity is not only in content but also in its deepest unconscious determinants a repetition of the pubertal constellations of the Oedipus complex; it is really an altered, modified new edition of the latter, or, let us say, an epilogue.

We shall not set out the case material here, but empirical observation has shown that the regressive trend of the climacteric libido breaks through the incest ban just as in puberty and that the objects subjected to that ban are cathected with new quantities of libido. For in the course of years only a transposition of the Oedipus complex has taken place, and not only as a result of neurotic applications of it on the one hand and normal developments on the other; the never-overcome incestuous fixations in their original form underwent a reactivation in relation to the children, who have now become objects of asexual love, just as the parents once were. As in the case of the latter, behind the pure affection lavished on the children large quantities of sexual components are concealed. I tried to describe above how in difficult sublimation work the ego ideal is re-erected in the son and how as a result of this task the son becomes an imago of the father. But the libidinal relationship that formerly applied to the father is also unconsciously transferred to the son.

The regressive over-cathexis of love of the son with its strong sexual emphasis is the typical destiny of the libido after the frustrations of the early climacteric that we described above.

This enables us to understand why the new edition of the rape fantasy expresses a masochistic attitude to the son. Its content is to be loved, seduced, beaten, murdered by him.

We see realizations of these fantasies in different versions of the mother–son relationship and in the relationship to son-in-law, daughter-in-law, etc. (Freud, 1912–13); the content of whore fantasies is the same as those of puberty, except that the son has taken the place of the father.

A patient who was suffering from menopausal difficulties and whose son was growing up imagined that she had a friend who in a spirit of heroic self-sacrifice tenderly introduced adolescent youths to the mysteries of sensual love. This fantasy was painted in the most glowing colours and soon betrayed the fact that the friend was the woman herself and that the young men stood for her son. In this connection I recall a dream noted by Dr Hermine von Hug-Hellmuth and used by Freud (1916–17, p. 136). The dreamer was a woman of fifty 'who day and night had no thought other than care for her child'. In the dream content she showed herself ready 'in fulfilment of a patriotic duty to offer herself for the satisfaction of the erotogenic needs of the military, officers and men alike'. This libidinal dream-fantasy seems to me to be identical with my patient's waking dream. Another hitherto healthy patient marked the outbreak for her neurosis with an anxiety dream that represented sexual intercourse with her son.

These incestuous relations of parents to their own children are revealed, as we have known for a long time, in the typical object-attractiveness of youths to ageing women and of adolescent girls to ageing men. We also know from the analysis of the neuroses that oedipal fixations are transferred by parents to their children. Thus a phenomenon I describe as typical of the menopause is merely a mobilization, a quantitative displacement in an already existing situation.

The reversion of the libido to objects subject to the incest prohibition that now sets in and the invasion of psychical life by unconscious fantasies lead to a characteristic personality change as well as numerous organic symptoms that generally have the quality of conversion formations.

The typical irritability of the unsatisfied, their liability to depression, numerous equivalents of anxiety—giddiness, palpitations, high pulse rates, etc.—closely resemble the numerous complaints that appear at puberty. In their unconscious content the depressions express the same thing as the menstrual depressions that frequently occur at puberty even among relatively healthy women. They are under the aegis of a double loss: that of the vaginal capacity of reproduction as well as the remobilized castration complex—in other words, an irrevocable blow to female narcissism.

Of the numerous organic symptoms such as headaches, neuralgia, vasomotor disturbances, heart sensations, digestive troubles, etc., a large number must be regarded as conversion symptoms, though the incipient dysfunction of the secretory glands as well as the beginning of organic involution produce a condition of organic readiness for them.

It is interesting to observe that it has been recently noted in non-psychological quarters that the physical symptoms of the menopause are strikingly reminiscent of those to be observed in the individuals concerned at puberty. Professor J. Wiesel, a Vienna specialist in internal diseases, writes in his paper on the internal symptomatology of the menopause in the *Manual of Female Biology and Pathology*: 'It has struck me that the disturbances of the gastro-intestinal tract, for instance, which come to our notice during puberty also introduce the menopause with extraordinary frequency, with quite similar symptoms in both cases. It can further be observed that in cases in which hyperthyroidism occurs at the age of development and later disappears without appearing again in the course of life, the menopause also begins under the aegis of hyperthyroidism. Or in cases in which changes in skin pigmentation appeared during puberty we see the same thing happening during the climacteric. The same applies to vasomotor disturbances, eczemas, anomalies of growth, etc. I had an interesting case of a patient in whom a thick lock of snow-white hair appeared during her years of development and subsequently disappeared, to reappear in the same place and in the same dimensions at the menopause.' Wiesel concludes: 'I wanted to show the large extent to which the symptomatology of puberty can be compared with events during the menopause.' I regard these purely somatic observations as a valuable confirmation of my views.

The phase of vaginal struggle and revived primacy of the clitoris is followed by a gradual transition to old age, with its pre-genital regressions, which manifest themselves both in character changes and in physical and psychical illnesses. Where to draw the line marking either the beginning or the end of the menopause is as difficult a problem from the psychological as it is from the organic point of view. The characteristic feature is generally held to be menstrual behaviour, though no-one has yet succeeded in demonstrating any characteristic anatomical limiting factor. Psychologically I would identify the beginning of the menopause with the phase of the struggle of the vagina to retain its primacy, or with the regression to the clitoris that we described above. This is certainly initiated by disturbances in the chemical and nervous correlation of the sexual processes—at the heart of which lies the incipient failure of the ovarial function. But the upheaval is demonstrated by psychical redispositions long before somatic factors manifest themselves. Like the somatologists, in normal physical conditions I would make the ending of the menopause coincide with the ending of menstruation. In my view menstruation demonstrates the existence of the genital function in the psychological sense also. The reciprocal dependence of psychical attitude on menstruation and of menstruation on libidinal processes perhaps acquires its greatest significance at this period of life. The following two cases may serve as examples.

A patient whose menstruations ceased for good at the age of thirty-five had the conscious feeling that this was connected with the approaching maturity of her son. Closer investigation confirmed her suspicion that her strongly libidinal relationship to her son and the fear of incest had caused her to take refuge in an early menopause.

A mentally ill lady in a late stage of the menopause, whom I was able to observe while acting on behalf of a colleague who was called to the colours during the war, preserved her menstruation for a strikingly long time for the benefit of that colleague—she lost it when he was called up and caused it to reappear at very irregular intervals when he visited her on leave. The content of the delusional ideas from which she suffered made it possible to establish the psychogenesis of this behaviour which, being hidden in the unconscious, would otherwise have not been so easy to explain.

The psychoneurotic events that take place in the phases of the early climacteric described above generally come under the heading of hysteria. Later pathological developments come under the pre-genital, that is to say the post-genital heading, i.e., they are obsessional, melancholic, paranoid.

The typical character changes of the age of involution, the depressive mood and the paranoid features, belong to the later post-genital (= pre-genital) phase, as do the so-called psychoses of involution, i.e., the typical melancholia and paranoia. Dispositional factors are responsible for the predominance of either anal or oral regression, and the same applies to the timing and intensity of these changes when they appear.

There are individuals in whom the genital climacteric phase is very soon succeeded by the post-genital phase, and *vice versa*. Also, two types of ageing in the physical and psychical respect can be distinguished, one of which is marked by oral regression while in the other anal regression predominates.

The factors that govern the choice of neurosis in individual cases must also be held responsible for the course taken by the menopause. Thus there are women who cope splendidly with the menopause or the genital phase and get into psychical difficulties only in subsequent regressions, or alternatively arrive at a peaceful haven in old age, after a stormy menopause.

At all events, the female change of life appears to be much more difficult than the male, and the different nature of the possibilities of sublimation open to the two sexes must be held largely responsible for this. While the woman's capacity for sublimation has to a large extent been absorbed by the reproductive function and succumbs to regression with the disappearance of the latter, man's capacity for sublimation survives much longer than his genital capacity.

Two ways lie open to woman to protect her against the disconsolateness of old age: the continuation of psychical motherhood in relation to the outside world or the now biologically revived bisexual constitution that frequently also emerges in the physical appearance of the ageing woman; by means of this, male-oriented relations to life can be maintained after the final disappearance of femininity.

The hope of therapeutic success for psychoanalysis at the age of involution is associated with these two possibilities.

An analysis begun just before the menopause or at the beginning of the difficulties caused by it could in my opinion do a great deal in the way of prophylaxis.

NOTE

1. Yet a strain of misogyny persists in a few psychoanalysts: as late as 1977 it was possible for an analyst to write: 'At present there seems to be a societal taboo against a frank discussion of areas of male superiority. It is evident that the male sex is superior not only in physical strength. I am referring to the surprising observation that mental achievements of a magnitude that is found in geniuses are almost always encountered in men and almost never in women. For this difference there must be a deep biological reason. The sociological explanation that is so frequently, if not regularly, heard can easily be disproved' (Eissler, 1977, p. 64).

REFERENCES

Abraham, K. (1922). Manifestation of the female castration complex. *International Journal of Psycho-Analysis, 3* (March).

————. (1945). A short study of the development of the libido. *Selected Papers* [reprinted London: Karnac Books, 1979].

Badinter, E. (1981). *Mother Love.* New York: Macmillan.

Baker, J. (1973). *Psychoanalysis and Women.* London: Penguin Books.

Barnett, M. C. (1966). Vaginal awareness in the infancy and childhood of girls. *Journal of the American Psychoanalytic Association, 14*: 129–141.

Bell, Q. (1972). *Virginia Woolf: A Biography, Vols. 1 & 2.* London: Hogarth.

Benedek, T. (1959). Sexual functions in women and their disturbances. In: S. Arieti (ed.), *American Handbook of Psychiatry, Vol. 1.* New York: Basic Books.

————. (1968). Discussion of Mary Jane Sherfey, *Journal of the American Psychoanalytic Association, 16*: 444.

Bibring, G. L., et al. (1961). A study of the psychological processes in pregnancy and of the earliest mother–child relationship. In: R. Eissler (ed.), *The Psychoanalytic Study of the Child, Vol. 16* (pp. 9–72). New York: International Universities Press.

Blum, H. P. (1976). Masochism, the ego ideal, and the psychology of women. *Journal of the American Psychoanalytic Association, 24* (Supplement): 157–191.

Bonaparte, M. (1935). Passivity, masochism and femininity. *International Journal of Psycho-Analysis, 16*: 325.

Brierley, M. (1932). Some problems of integration in women. *International Journal of Psycho-Analysis, 13*: 437.

——— . (1936). Specific determinants in feminine development. *International Journal of Psycho-Analysis, 17*: 163–180.

Brownmiller, S. (1975). *Against Our Will*. New York: Simon & Schuster.

Chasseguet-Smirgel, J. (1976). Freud and female sexuality. *International Journal of Psycho-Analysis, 57*: 275–286.

Chesler, P. (1972). *Women and Madness*. New York: Doubleday.

Chodorow, N. (1978). *The Reproduction of Mothering*. Berkeley, CA: University of California Press.

de Beauvoir, S. (1961). *The Second Sex*. New York: Bantam.

Deutsch, H. (1944). *The Psychology of Women, Vol. 1*. New York: Grune & Stratton.

——— . (1945). *The Psychology of Women, Vol. 2*. New York: Grune & Stratton.

——— . (1948a). The psychology of women in relation to the functions of reproduction. In: R. Fliess (ed.), *The Psychoanalytic Reader* (pp. 165–179). New York: International Universities Press.

——— . (1948b). The significance of masochism in the mental life of women. In: R. Fliess (ed.), *The Psychoanalytic Reader* (pp. 195–207). New York: International Universities Press.

——— . (1965). *Neuroses and Character Types*. New York: International Universities Press.

——— . (1967). *Selected Problems in Adolescence*. New York: International Universities Press.

——— . (1973). *Confrontations with Myself*. New York: Norton.

Eisler, J. M. (1923). Über hysterischen Erscheinungen am Uterus. *Internationale Zeitschrift für Psychoanalyse*: 266ff.

Eissler, K. R. (1977). Comments on penis envy and orgasm in women. In: R. Eissler (ed.), *The Psychoanalytic Study of the Child, Vol. 32*. New Haven, CT: Yale University Press.

Erikson, E. H. (1963). *Childhood and Society*, second ed. New York: Norton.

————— . (1980). On the generational cycle. *International Journal of Psycho-Analysis, 61*: 213–223.

Fenichel, O. (1931). The pregenital antecedents of the Oedipus complex. *International Journal of Psycho-Analysis, 12*.

Fenichel, O. (1933). Outline of clinical psychoanalysis. *Psychoanalytic Quarterly, 2*.

————— . (1945). *The Psychoanalytic Theory of Neurosis*. New York: Norton.

Ferenczi, S. (1938). *Thalassa: A Theory of Genitality*. New York: Psychoanalytic Quarterly; reprinted 1989 London: Karnac Books.

Fliegel, Z. O. (1973). Feminine psychosexual development in Freudian theory. *Psychoanalytic Quarterly, 42*: 385–408.

Freud, S. (1905d). Three essays on the theory of sexuality. *Standard Edition, 7*.

————— . (1909a [1908]). Some general remarks on hysterical attacks. *Standard Edition, 9*.

————— . (1910h). A special type of choice of object made by men. *Standard Edition, 11*.

————— . (1912d). On the universal tendency to debasement in the sphere of love. *Standard Edition, 11*.

————— . (1912f). Contributions to a discussion on masturbation. *Standard Edition, 12*.

————— . (1912–13). Totem and taboo. *Standard Edition, 13*.

————— . (1916–17). Introductory lectures; Lecture 9. *Standard Edition, 15*.

————— . (1917c). On transformations of instinct as exemplified in anal erotism. *Standard Edition, 17*.

————— . (1918a). The taboo of virginity. *Standard Edition, 11*.

————— . (1918b [1914]). From the history of an infantile neurosis. *Standard Edition, 17*.

————— . (1923e). The infantile genital organisation. *Standard Edition, 19*.

————— . (1924d). The dissolution of the Oedipus complex. *Standard Edition, 19*.

————— . (1924c). The economic problem of masochism. *Standard Edition, 19*.

————— . (1925j). Some psychical consequences of the anatomical distinction between the sexes. *Standard Edition, 19*.

————— . (1931b). Female sexuality. *Standard Edition, 21*.

———— . (1933a [1932]). New Introductory Lectures on Psycho-analysis. *Standard Edition, 22.*

———— . (1950–74). *Standard Edition of the Complete Works of Sigmund Freud.* London: Hogarth Press.

———— . (1954). *The Origins of Psychoanalysis.* Marie Bonaparte, Anna Freud, Ernst Kris (eds.), translated by Eric Mosbacher and James Strachey. London: Imago.

Friday, N. (1977). *My Mother/My Self.* New York: Delacorte.

Friedan, B. (1963). *The Feminine Mystique.* New York: Norton, 1963.

Fromm, E. (1963). Sex and character. *The Dogma of Christ* (pp. 107–127). New York: Holt, Rinehart & Winston.

Gagnon, J. H. (1965). Sexuality and sexual learning in the child. *Psychiatry, 28*: 212–228.

———— . (1977). *Human Sexualities.* Glenview, IL: Scott, Foresman.

Galenson, E. (1976). Panel report on the psychology of women. *Journal of the American Psychoanalytic Association, 24*: 141–160.

Garrison, D. (1981). Karen Horney and Feminism. *Signs, 6*: 672–691.

Gilman, R. (1971). The femlib case against Sigmund Freud. *The New York Times Magazine,* 31 January, pp. 10–11, 42, 44, 47.

Gordon, S. (1978). Helene Deutsch and the legacy of Freud. *The New York Times Magazine,* 30 July.

Greer, G. (1970). *The Female Eunuch.* London: MacGibbon & Kee.

Groddeck, G. (1961). *The Book of the It.* New York: Vintage.

Harnik, J. (1923). Schicksale des Narzissmuss beim Mann und Weib. *Internationale Zeitschrift für Psychoanalyse, 9*: 278ff.

Hitschmann, E. (1932). A ten years' report of the Vienna Psycho-analytic Clinic. *International Journal of Psycho-Analysis, 13.*

———— . (1954). Letter to Ernest Jones, 26 March. Jones Archives.

Holroyd, M. (1967–68). *Lytton Strachey: A Critical Biography, Vols. 1 & 2.* London: William Heinemann.

Horney, K. (1924). On the genesis of the castration complex in women. *International Journal of Psycho-analysis, 5.*

———— . (1926). Book Review of H. Deutsch, *Psychoanalysis of the Sexual Functions of Women, International Journal of Psycho-Analysis, 7*: 92–100.

————. (1967). 'The flight from womanhood' and 'The denial of the vagina'. In: H. Kelman (ed.), *Female Psychology*. New York: Norton.

————. (1973). *Feminine Psychology*. New York: Norton.

Jacobson, E. (1976). Ways of female superego formation and the female castration complex. *Psychoanalytic Quarterly, 45*.

Jones, E. (1961). The early development of female sexuality. In: *Papers on Psychoanalysis*. Boston, MA: Beacon Press; reprinted 1977 London: Karnac Books.

Kardiner, A. (1977). *My Analysis with Freud*. New York: Norton.

Kardiner, A., Karush, A., & Ovesey, L. (1959). A methodological study of Freudian theory: III. Narcissism, bisexuality and the dual instinct theory. *Journal of Nervous and Mental Disease, 129*: 207–221.

Kehrer, E. (1922). *Ursachen und Behandlung der Unfruchtbarkeit*.

Kestenberg, J. S. (1956). Vicissitudes of female sexuality. *Journal of the American Psychoanalytic Association, 4*.

Kitzinger, S. (1978). *The Experience of Childbirth*, 4th ed. London: Penguin Books.

Klein, M. (1950). Early stages of the Oedipus conflict. In: *Contributions to Psychoanalysis*. London: Hogarth Press.

————. (1960). *The Psychoanalysis of Children*. New York: Grove Press.

Koff, E., Rierdan, J., & Jacobson, S. (1981). The personal and interpersonal significance of menarche. *The Journal of the American Academy of Child Psychiatry, 20*: 148–158.

Lampl-de Groot, J. (1948). The evolution of the Oedipus complex in women. In: R. Fliess (ed.), *The Psychoanalytic Reader*. New York: International Universities Press.

Lasch, C. (1974). Freud and women. *New York Review of Books, 3* October, pp. 12–17.

Leiblum, S., & Pervin, L. (1980). *Principles and Practice of Sex Therapy*. New York: Guilford Press.

Lorand, S. (1939). The problem of vaginal orgasm. *International Journal of Psycho-Analysis, 20*: 432–438.

Marmor, J. (1954). Some considerations concerning orgasm in the female. *Psychosomatic Medicine, 16*: 240–265.

Miller, J. B. (1973). *Psychoanalysis and Women*. London: Penguin Books.

————. (1976). *Toward a New Psychology of Women*. Boston, MA: Beacon Press.

Millet, K. (1971). *Sexual Politics*. New York: Avon.

Mitchell, J. (1974). *Psychoanalysis and Feminism*. New York: Pantheon.

Money, J., & Ehrhardt, A. (1973). *Man and Woman, Boy and Girl*. Baltimore: Johns Hopkins University Press.

Nagera, H. (1975). *Female Sexuality and the Oedipus Complex*. New York: Jason Aronson.

————. (1976). Supplement—Female psychology. *Journal of the American Psychoanalytic Association, 24.*

Payne, S. M. (1935). A conception of femininity. *The British Journal of Medical Psychology, 15.*

Quinn, S. (1987). *A Mind of Her Own: The Life of Karen Horney*. New York: Summit Books.

Rado, S. (1928). The psychical effects of intoxication. *International Journal of Psycho-Analysis, 9*: 315.

————. (1940). A critical examination of the concept of bisexuality. *Psychosomatic Medicine, 2*: 459–467.

Rank, O. (1929). *The Trauma of Birth*. New York: Harcourt Brace.

Rank, O., & Ferenczi, S. (1956). *The Development of Psycho-analysis*. New York: Dover Publications.

Reich, W. (1970). *The Mass Psychology of Fascism*. New York: Farrar, Straus & Giroux.

————. (1975). The impulsive character. *Early Writings*. New York: Farrar, Straus & Giroux.

Reik, T. (1914). Die Couvade. In: *Probleme der Religionspsychologie, Part I*. Internationale Psychoanalytische Bibliothek.

Reinach (n.d.). *Cultes, Mythes et Religions: Une Mystique au XVIIième Siècle.*

Reitz, R. (1979). *Menopause*. London: Penguin Books.

Riviere, J. (1934). Book Review: S. Freud, *New Introductory Lectures on Psycho-Analysis. International Journal of Psycho-Analysis, 15*: 329–339.

Roazen, P. (1975). *Freud and His Followers*. New York: Knopf [reprinted New York: New York University Press, 1985].

————. (1969). *Brother Animal: The Story of Freud and Tausk.*

New York: Knopf. Second edition with new Introduction, New York: Transaction, 1990.

————. (1976). *Erik H. Erikson: The Power and Limits of a Vision.* New York: The Free Press.

————. (1985). *Helene Deutsch: A Psychoanalyst's Life.* New York: Doubleday/Anchor.

————. (1990). *Encountering Freud: The Politics and Histories of Psychoanalysis.* New York: Transaction.

Robinson, P. (1976). *The Modernization of Sex.* New York: Harper & Row.

Rubins, J. L. (1978). *Karen Horney.* New York: Dial Press.

Schafer, R. (1974). Problems in Freud's psychology of women. *Journal of the American Psychoanalytic Association, 22*: 459–485.

Searl, M. N. (1938). A note on the relation between physical and psychical differences in boys and girls. *International Journal of Psycho-Analysis, 19*: 52.

Sherfey, M. J. (1972). *The Nature and Evolution of Female Sexuality.* New York: Random House.

Stoller, R. J. (1974). Facts and fancies: An examination of Freud's concept of bisexuality. In: J. Strouse (ed.), *Women and Analysis* (pp. 343–364). New York: Grossman.

Sturgis, S., et al. (1962). *The Gynecologic Patient: A Psycho-Endocrine Study.* New York: Grune & Stratton.

Trilling, L. (1957). The Kinsey Report. In: *The Liberal Imagination* (pp. 216–235). New York: Anchor.

Webster, B. S. (1985). Helene Deutsch: A new look. *Signs, 10*, No. 3 (Spring), p. 562.

Wiesel, J. (n.d.). *Manual of Female Biology and Pathology.*